A Spectator's Guide to
Jesus

A Lion Book
an imprint of
Lion Hudson plc
Wilkinson House, Jordan Hill Road,
Oxford OX2 8DR, England
www.lionhudson.com
ISBN 978 0 8254 6253 5 (USA)
ISBN 978 0 7459 5307 6 (UK)

First published in 2005 by Blue Bottle Books,
PO Box A287, Sydney South, Australia 1235

First Lion edition 2008
10 9 8 7 6 5 4 3 2 1 0

A catalogue record for this book is available
from the British Library

Typeset in 11/13 Latin 725 BT
Printed and bound in the USA

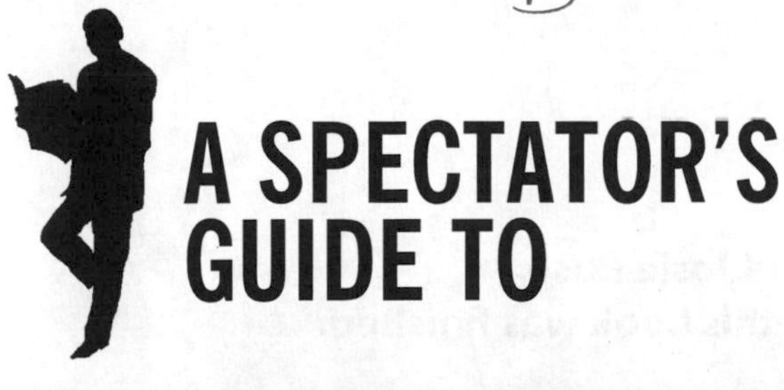

A SPECTATOR'S GUIDE TO JESUS

An Introduction to the Man from Nazareth

JOHN DICKSON

For my beautiful Josie Rose,
born the week this book was finished.

Contents

Contents

Foreword
Peter Garrett MP

It is too obvious to say that the figure of Jesus has intrigued, absorbed and inspired devotion in millions of people through the ages, but central to the figure of Jesus is the simple fact – devoid of national, religious or cultural clothing – of universal fascination with the teacher from Galilee.

John Dickson's masterly but accessible account goes some way to explaining this phenomenon by stripping away the myths and the religiosity that often obscure the Jesus people followed over 2000 years ago, and still follow today.

For someone coming to the Jesus story fresh – and what better way is there? – the overwhelming impression is of a person centred in a place that, while possible to imagine, is impossible to fully understand; indeed, the stories in the Gospels are very clear on that score. No one really knew what he was on about, at least not at the time, and not fully. Talk about mystery!

It is not simply the exceeding-natural-laws part of Jesus' life that inspires either incredulity or amazement, depending on your take; it's also the discernible calm of someone literally at the centre of the storm. Leave aside the many romanticized versions of Jesus, in art and film and Sunday school, and you come up against Jesus living as a wanderer, dying as a criminal, run down by a rough and cruel invading power and left to the mercies of the state by the religious leaders of the day.

The message then, as now, was a tough one: love your enemies, welcome the return of the wayward son, sit down with the scum of the earth and celebrate the bounty of creation, the poor are blessed, and you love your God by aiming true.

The most profound challenge of Jesus' life is that it is still lived; the great attraction of his story – his history – is that we can tap into it as we too live our lives. And this book is a fine way to start that.

Foreword

Introduction
Jesus of the imagination

Some readers will have heard before the famous story of the young lads who stepped onto a bus in the US in thc mid 1930s and tried to pick a fight with a man sitting up the back by himself. They began with a few light insults. The stranger did not respond. They sat closer and turned up the heat of the insults and still he said nothing.

A few minutes passed before they arrived at the man's stop. He stood up – he was much bigger than they had estimated! He looked down at the young men, reached into his pocket and handed them his card. He turned and quietly got off the bus and walked on his way.

The lads huddled around the card, eager to learn the name of this gentle giant. They read the words: 'Joe Louis, Professional Boxer'.

For those who do not know their boxing history, it turns out these young men had just tried to start a fight with the man who would become the Heavyweight Boxing Champion of the World from 1937–1949, one of the most successful pugilists of all time. Their assumptions about the stranger were all wrong: the business card, not to mention the events of the next few years, proved just how wrong.

This reportedly true story illustrates a common occurrence in the modern approach to the subject of this book, Jesus. Either through misinformation, wishful thinking or prejudice – and sometimes a combination of all three – the Jesus of public imagination is often markedly different from the figure we find in our earliest sources. Our assumptions prove misleading.

The Jesus of public imagination

When I say 'public imagination' I include here the imagination of the Christian Church. Although I write as a participant in mainstream Christianity, I am frequently struck by the difference between the Christ preached in some contemporary sermons and the man who emerges from the pages of history. Indeed, somewhere deep inside my computer's hard drive are numerous sermons I have preached in the past but, for reasons that will become clear in the following pages, I could no longer deliver with the same sincerity.

Equally questionable are some of the assumed Jesuses in popular discourse. The Dan Brown novel *The Da Vinci Code* offers one obvious example. Here, fictional experts effortlessly strip back the ecclesiastically conspired 'Son of God' to reveal the true man, a simple, wise teacher who settled down with a wife and kids and whose descendants can be found living happily in modern France.

Brown's Jesus is admittedly a soft target (more about that later). Other imaginary Jesuses carry an air of plausibility. Take Mel Gibson's *The Passion of the Christ,* complete with dialogue in Aramaic and Latin, the languages of Jesus and the Romans respectively.[1] I must admit, I was deeply moved by the film and found it very realistic: those who criticized Gibson for 'exaggerating' the sufferings of Christ need to remember that scourging and crucifixion were intentionally horrifying modes of punishment in the Roman world (more about that in Chapter 9). Nevertheless, the Jesus that emerged from Gibson's portrayal was, despite the attempted realism, a rather one-dimensional figure. He was a mere sacrificial lamb on its way to slaughter. There is of course a truth here, as any first year theology student will tell you, but it is a 'truth' devoid of historical context and detached from the extraordinary life that preceded this suffering and gives it its proper meaning. My atheist friend had a point when he said that, without an appreciation of what Jesus said and did, watching the poor guy get beaten to a pulp for two hours was anything but spiritually enlightening.

The Jesus of academic imagination

Some of the *academic* images of Jesus are equally open to criticism. Readers may be surprised to learn that scholarly books and articles on the 'historical Jesus' number in the tens of thousands. A vast industry has emerged in the last 30 years dedicated to uncovering the *real* Jesus – as opposed, it is thought, to the Christ of the Church.

Typically, however, the only studies to attract public attention are the 'sensational' ones – those that contradict mainstream perspectives on Christ. These studies hit the headlines and make their way into documentaries. The viewing public is left understandably perplexed and unaware that most of the best scholarship never reaches them.

I have explored this in detail in another book,[2] but it is worth repeating here. It is a sad fact of scholarship (in many academic fields) that the most impressive work is too subtle, cautious and sophisticated (i.e. boring) to be considered newsworthy by the regular media outlets. The headline 'Jesus overturned first-century dining rules' is hardly going to excite a newspaper editor, even though it is based on solid data. The headline 'Jesus was gay', on the other hand, will cause a small media storm, even if it is based on the musings of an astrologer, a PhD student and a gay activist.[3]

This highlights something that is well worth knowing about the scholarly game. In any field of academia, especially in New Testament studies it seems, scholarship tends to fall into three broad camps, or three points along a continuum. Somewhere out on the left-hand margin is *sceptical* scholarship. Experts here ply the scholarly craft in the service of nay-saying and hyper-scepticism. They relish offering new theories that call into question the results of broader scholarship.[4] On the opposite margin is *apologetic* scholarship, in which experts focus mainly on defending traditional Christianity from scepticism.[5] They often take their cue, in fact, from sceptical scholarship. Like sceptical scholars, most apologists have good credentials but they tend to bypass the normal process of academic review and publish directly for the public.

Between these two margins is what you might call *mainstream* or *middle* scholarship. This is where the majority of professional scholars are to be found. Mainstream scholars rarely hit the headlines or the shelves of popular bookstores, but they are regularly published in the hundred or so major peer review journals dedicated to the subject area.[6]

On the whole, mainstream scholars are little interested in debunking or defending Christianity; they are neither staunch sceptics nor devout apologists. They just get on with the business of analyzing the New Testament and related material in the way historians treat any other comparable historical source from the period: whether Caesar, Seneca or Tacitus on the Latin side, or Plutarch, Epictetus or Lucian on the Greek.

The approach of *A Spectator's Guide*

Let me hasten to add that I have no delusions about where along this spectrum of scholarship the current book lies: frankly, nowhere. This is not an academic work and I do not wish to suggest to readers that what follows is a careful distillation of the current scholarly debate about Jesus. My goals and approach are quite different.

Nevertheless, in what follows I intend to keep within the bounds not of the marginal but of the mainstream. While I am personally sympathetic to the aims of apologetic scholars, I have drawn almost nothing from them in writing this book. Needless to say, I have drawn little from sceptical scholarship either.

At times this will mean I have to be circumspect about things I actually believe to be true. For instance, when I mention the unavoidable topic of Jesus' reported miracles, readers will notice that I make no attempt to prove Jesus did in fact heal the sick, restore the blind and so on. This is not because I do not accept these things; it is simply because I think the historical sources are incapable of proving (or disproving) things like healings. In this, and many other instances, I find the assessment of mainstream scholars more realistic as a historical conclusion: while historians cannot say Jesus *actually* healed the sick, they can, and generally do, say that Jesus did things which those around him believed to be miraculous.[7] Whether or not you and I concur with this belief depends not on historical considerations but on philosophical assumptions (such as what we regard as *possible* in the universe). More about this later.

The aim of *A Spectator's Guide to Jesus* is to provide readers with an introduction to the major portraits of Jesus found in the earliest historical sources. I say 'portraits' (in the plural) because our best information points not to a tidy, monolithic Jesus but to a complex, multi-layered and, at times, contradictory figure (compare Chapters 12 and 13). To recall my Joe Louis story, the 'business cards' of Jesus are many and varied; hence the chapter headings of this book.

Some might be troubled by this, supposing that plurality equals incomprehensibility or unreliability. Others take it as an invitation to do a little rearranging for themselves, trying to make Jesus neater, more digestible (this tends to be the work of theologians). Then there are those, and I admit to being one of them, who quite like the idea that after two millennia of spiritual devotion and more than two centuries of modern critical research we still cannot fit this figure into a single box. Jesus, it seems, is destined to stretch our imaginations, confront our beliefs and challenge our lifestyles for many years to come.

A book like this, then, will have done its job properly only if its readers – along with its author – find themselves disturbed as much as intrigued by the images of Jesus found in the sources. Conscious of this evocative dimension of the figure of Jesus I have tried throughout the book to give readers an idea of how these portraits of Christ have influenced church, society and the individual, both ancient and modern. Each chapter ends with a Reflections section. These should not be read as 'homilies' designed to put readers on the spot. They are an attempt to highlight how, through the ages, believers and unbelievers alike have found themselves confronted and/or inspired by these particular images of Jesus. While it is true that people have fashioned versions of Christ into their own digestible image, it is equally true that the figure of Jesus has exerted an enormous influence over those who have pondered his life and teaching. I say this as a personal statement as much as a description of the plan of the book.

We begin with the obvious first question: how do we know what we know about Jesus? What are the sources, both direct and indirect, of our knowledge of the man?

1 Sources
How we know what we know about Jesus

Unlike the Hindu Upanishads, which focus on the believer's merger with the life force Brahman, or the Buddhist Tripitaka, which emphasizes the extinguishment of self and suffering, or the Islamic Qur'an, which centres on the nature and practice of submission to God, the New Testament revolves around a series of events said to have occurred in Palestine between 5 BC and AD 30. This makes Christianity particularly open – perhaps vulnerable – to historical scrutiny. The logic is simple: if you claim that something spectacular took place in history, intelligent people are going to ask you historical questions. Christianity has, on the whole, welcomed this. It is as if the Christian faith places its head on the chopping block of public scrutiny and invites us all to take a swing. And, so far, Christianity has fared well.

Jesus arrived on the scene at a time of great literary activity. Philosophers were writing weighty tomes on the meaning of life. Poets and playwrights were composing material to make people laugh and cry. Emperors were crafting royal propaganda to ensure they were well remembered. And historians were recording for posterity all that they could discover about the startling events surrounding the rise of the Roman Empire. The non-biblical writings from this period (100 BC – AD 200) fill many shelves in your local university library.

One lucky outcome of this flurry of ancient literary output is that a small town Jewish teacher, named Yeshua ben Yosef, or

Jesus son of Joseph, happened to rate a mention in several of the writings of the period. This is not as predictable as you might imagine. Although today we recognize Jesus as the founder of the world's largest religion,[8] back in the first century he was hardly known at all outside the tiny strip of Roman ruled land called Palestine. It is a sheer and happy accident of history that Jesus rated a mention outside the texts of the New Testament (a selection of readings from these non-Christian sources can be found at the end of this chapter).[9]

Our direct sources of information about Jesus come from three sets of ancient writings: Greco-Roman, Jewish and Christian.

Greco-Roman references to Jesus

Jesus is mentioned in passing on numerous occasions in the writings of Greeks and Romans in the period following his death. The list includes the following:

1. The pagan historian Thallos, around AD 55, in the third volume of his *Histories*, mentions a darkness coinciding with the crucifixion of Jesus. He describes it as a natural eclipse of the sun and not a supernatural event of significance.
2. The stoic writer Mara bar Serapion, shortly after AD 70, refers to Jesus as a king and teacher and compares him to the Greek martyrs Pythagoras and Socrates.
3. The Roman historian Cornelius Tacitus (AD 56–120) scathingly refers to Jesus' execution under Pontius Pilate and describes the movement surrounding him as a 'deadly superstition'.
4. The Roman administrator Pliny the Younger (AD 61–113) mentions the early Christian worship of Jesus 'as a god'.
5. The Roman historian Suetonius, around AD 120, refers to disturbances among Roman Jews (of which there were thousands) over the claim that Jesus was the 'Christ' (i.e. the Jewish Messiah).
6. The Greek satirist, Lucian of Samosata (AD 115–200), ridicules Jesus as a 'crucified sophist'.

7. The Greek intellectual Celsus, around AD 175, insists Jesus' conception was suspect and his miracles mere Egyptian magic.

Jewish references to Jesus

Jesus is mentioned on four occasions in Jewish writings of the first and second centuries:

1. The first-century historian Josephus recounts Jesus' fame as a teacher, healer and martyr. Jesus' resurrection is said to have been 'reported' by his followers.
2. In another text the same writer recounts the martyrdom of a man called James, whom Josephus describes as the 'brother of Jesus the so-called Messiah'. The same brother, incidentally, appears frequently in the New Testament.[10]
3. The Talmud, an ancient exposition of Jewish law, contains a passage (dated AD 100–200) justifying Jesus' execution at the time of the Jewish Passover on the grounds that he 'led Israel astray' and 'practised sorcery'.
4. In a later text (post AD 200) the Talmud also insists that Jesus' mother, Mary, was an adulteress.

Piecing it all together

These Greco-Roman and Jewish references provide little more than an outline of Jesus' life. They are too brief and cursory to be of value in reconstructing a 'life of Jesus'. Some of the passages were written too late to be of much historical value at all (e.g. the second Talmudic reference just mentioned). Nevertheless, it is worth listing the handful of details about Jesus we may glean from these non-Christian texts:

1. The name 'Jesus'.
2. The place and time-frame of his public ministry (Palestine during Pontius Pilate's governorship, AD 26–36).
3. The name of his mother (Mary).

4. The ambiguous nature of his birth.
5. The name of one of his brothers (James).
6. His fame as a teacher.
7. His fame as a miracle-worker/sorcerer.
8. The attribution to him of the title 'Messiah/Christ'.
9. His 'kingly' status in the eyes of some.
10. The time and manner of his execution (crucifixion around the time of the Passover festival).
11. The involvement of both the Roman and Jewish leadership in his death.
12. The coincidence of an eclipse at the time of his crucifixion.
13. The report of Jesus' appearances to his followers after his death.
14. The flourishing of a movement that worshipped Jesus after his death.

Obviously, nothing can be gained from the above about, say, what Jesus stood for, what he expected from his followers or what drove him to the path of martyrdom. For these details we have to turn to the third and most important direct source of information about Jesus – the writings of the New Testament.

Christian writings about Jesus

Recently, I was talking to a highly intelligent woman who asked me about the sources of our knowledge of Jesus. I took her through the Greco-Roman and Jewish sources and then began to list the Christian ones. She stopped me and said, 'But surely you can't use those. They were all written by religious believers.' She somehow got it into her head that religious devotion disqualified religious texts from being considered as historical data.

Let me begin, then, by clearing up two major misunderstandings about the writings of the early Christians. Firstly, the so-called 'religious' nature of Christian writings in no way diminishes their value as historical sources. It is true that historians take the Christian agenda into account when they analyze the New Testament writings, just as they do the biases in Tacitus and Josephus, but it is not the case that historians place Christian writings in a special category. Professional scholars approach the New Testament as they would any other first-century text. They do not treat it as the Word of God, as the Christian Church does, but they do accord it the status of a valuable historical text. In fact, it is no exaggeration to say that historians universally regard the New Testament writings (no matter what their persuasion) as the earliest, most plentiful and most reliable sources of information about the Jesus of history.[11]

The second thing to say is that the New Testament is not a single source at all; it is a collection of sources. In the discipline known as 'theology' (the study of God's nature and activity), the Bible is appropriately treated as one homogenous source – all ultimately coming from God. Passages from one biblical writer are placed seamlessly next to passages from another in order to build up a coherent picture of the divine character and intentions. Sermons in church normally use Scripture in the same way. In historical research, however, the New Testament is analyzed as a compilation of *independent* traditions with common convictions about Jesus of Nazareth. Christians need to remember that, although our sacred documents were composed and circulated in the first century, they were not brought together into a single volume (the New Testament) until the fourth century.[12] Before that time these texts had lives of their own, you might say.

Let me give you a few examples. The apostle Paul, who wrote numerous documents now in the New Testament, never knew, for instance, the Gospel of Mark (and Mark never knew Paul's letters either). Historians therefore treat his epistles as a source *separate* from that of Mark. Again, the Gospel of John was composed *independently* of the Gospel of Matthew, so these individual Gospels represent another set of separate sources. James – the brother of Jesus mentioned earlier – did not know any of these Gospels, so his letter constitutes yet another source.

There are even sources *within* the Gospels, which historians treat as earlier independent traditions pulled together into a later text, much the same way as Tacitus drew together prior sources in his famous Roman *Annals*. The Gospel of Luke, for instance, relies on at least three sources recognized by scholars: (1) the Gospel of Mark written probably ten years before Luke; (2) a document dubbed 'Q' which contained numerous sayings of Jesus; and (3) a source called 'L' which was a collection of parables and other reports about Jesus. Luke himself in the opening paragraph of his Gospel mentions his investigation of prior sources:

> *Many have undertaken to draw up an account of the things that have been fulfilled among us, just as they were handed down to us by those who from the first were eyewitnesses and servants of the word. Therefore, since I myself have carefully investigated everything from the beginning, it seemed good also to me to write an orderly account for you, most excellent Theophilus [probably his patron], so that you may know the certainty of the things you have been taught.*
> ***Luke 1:1–3***

Whatever else this is, it is a claim to be writing as a historian about historical events using prior historical sources. Although not motivated by this claim, the modern identification of Luke's sources (as Mark, Q and L) is entirely consistent with what Luke himself affirms. Other recognized sources for the study of Jesus within the New Testament include 'M', Signs Source (SQ), the letters of Paul and the epistle of James (the brother of Jesus).[13]

To the general public, the fact that several parts of the New Testament say the same thing about Jesus does not seem all that significant. This is because most of us, if we ponder these things at all, are used to thinking about the New Testament as a single document. Historians view it quite differently. The fact that Paul, Mark, Q and L independently offer strikingly similar descriptions of Jesus' life and teaching is highly significant. Because we know these sources are not copied from each other, we have to assume their information was both early and widely known. This is a basic principle of historical study. The *criterion of multiple attestation*, as it is known, says that when numerous ancient sources independently offer roughly the same portrait of an event or person, that portrait takes on greater plausibility. It is the same logic you would apply to some surprising news from friends. If the same news came from two or three different friends (and you knew they had not colluded), you are far more likely to take them at their word.

Background sources

So far we have been discussing the direct sources about Jesus. There are also what you might call background sources. These are writings from the period that shed indirect light on the political, religious and cultural context of Jesus' life. They provide the canvas on which our picture of Jesus can more realistically be painted. I will be drawing on many of these throughout the book.

1. The most obvious 'background' source for the study of Jesus is the *Tanakh*, or what Christians call the Old Testament.[14] Historians are generally agnostic about whether Jesus fulfilled the Old Testament prophecies concerning a coming Messiah – as Christians affirm – but they do agree the Tanakh provides one of the richest backgrounds for an accurate understanding of his message and conduct. We will meet the Old Testament many more times in this book.
2. The *Dead Sea Scrolls* provide a fascinating account of purity rules among Jews of Jesus' day. Although they say nothing about Jesus directly (for the most part, they were written in the century before Christ), they do reveal just how radical Jesus' friendships with lepers, sinners and women must have seemed to many of his contemporaries in Palestine.
3. The *Mishnah* is a collection of the sayings of about 150 Jewish rabbis from the first and second centuries. When

these words are set against the sayings of Jesus, we begin to get a sense of how outrageous some of his teachings were in the eyes of his contemporaries. A striking example will be offered in the next chapter.

4. I have already mentioned the multi-volume history of the Jews by Josephus. The main significance of these writings is not that they mention Jesus on a couple of occasions, but that they tell us much about the anti-Roman resistance movements Jesus must have been critiquing when he said to his countrymen things like 'love your enemies' and 'pray for those who mistreat you'.[15]

5. The Jewish *Pseudepigrapha* contains sermons, novels and letters written by Jewish leaders in the centuries before and after Jesus. One of the fascinating things they reveal is the kind of Messiah Jews in the period were hoping for. As we shall see in Chapter 5, Jesus hardly fits the expected job description.

6. Roman writers such as Tacitus, Suetonius, Pliny and Seneca all reveal the economic and political realities that Jesus and his fellow Palestinians had to endure in the first century. They also make clear why the Romans would have felt such contempt for the preposterous claim that a crucified Jew was the true Caesar of the world, a theme explored in Chapter 11.

7. To these literary sources can be added the findings of archaeology. As you are reading this, scores of 'digs' are going on all around the Mediterranean. Some of them are yielding important results for the study of Jesus. The discovery of Jesus' hometown of Nazareth, for example, has enabled us to build up a picture of the close-knit, traditional Jewish community in which he grew up.

8. The final background sources to mention are the so-called 'apocryphal Gospels', works penned a century or more after the New Testament. These include the Gospel of Thomas, the Gospel of Philip, the Gospel of Mary Magdalene and many others. I mention these here not because they tell us anything about the Jesus of history but because in recent years a rumour has emerged that

> the four New Testament Gospels (Matthew, Mark, Luke and John) were officially accepted only very late in the piece and that various *other* Gospels were secretly excluded, all for devious political reasons. Something like this was described in Dan Brown's *The Da Vinci Code*.[16]
>
> In reality, the four New Testament Gospels, all written in the first century, unwittingly spawned a virtual Gospel-writing industry in the second and third centuries. As Christianity spread throughout the Mediterranean world various splinter groups began to imitate, extend and sometimes re-write the older teachings of Jesus. They produced their own Gospels in the names of former biblical greats (such as Thomas, Philip, Mary Magdalene and so on). That way, they could mount a claim that Jesus himself had taught their idiosyncratic views. Historians treat these extra 'Gospels' not as sources for our knowledge of the historical Jesus, but as testimony to the variety of responses to the figure of Christ a century or two later.[17]

Taken together these direct and indirect, Christian and non-Christian sources provide (with the exception of the apocryphal Gospels) a wealth of information about Jesus Christ. The picture that emerges from the data, as I hope to show throughout this book, is both deeply credible and profoundly counter-intuitive. As one of Australia's most celebrated ancient historians wrote:

> *An ancient historian has no problem seeing the phenomenon of Jesus as an historical one. His many surprising aspects only help anchor him in history. Myth or legend would have created a more predictable figure. The writings that sprang up about Jesus also reveal to us a movement of thought and an experience of life so unusual that something much more substantial than the imagination is needed to explain it.*[18]

Let me close with three brief reflections.

Reflections

1. *The nature of Christian Scripture.* There is something quite instructive in all this about the distinctive nature of the Christian New Testament when compared with the Scriptures of other world faiths. The Islamic holy book the Qur'an, for instance, is said to be a direct revelation from God entirely devoid of human participation in its composition. It is believed to be a perfect copy of a 'Mother Qur'an' stored in heaven. The prophet Muhammad merely *recited* what was divinely dictated to him (*qur'an* means 'recitation'). The earliest and most sacred portion of the Hindu Scriptures, the Vedas, are likewise believed to have been eternally and divinely disclosed.

Christian Scripture is quite different. The books of the New Testament have always presented themselves, in the first instance, as *historical* texts. They are *letters* written to specific social settings and *biographies* based on earlier sources. Does this observation undermine the Christian belief that the New Testament is also the Word of God? Not at all. From the very beginning, Christians treated their sacred documents as both human and divine. Just as Christian theology has had no problem thinking of Jesus as both God and man, so the church has (usually) had no hesitation affirming the New Testament as both a divinely inspired text and a truly historical text. Christianity is a historical faith based not on a divine dictation or a private revelation but on public events that are, for better or worse, open to public scrutiny.

2. *Christian confidence.* Christians often take the front foot on questions of the credibility of Jesus and the writings of the New Testament. Although they sometimes go too far – there is a fine line between confidence and arrogance – they are right to insist that after two centuries of modern critical scrutiny the basic plot of Christ's life recounted in the Gospels holds firm.

While newspapers will occasionally report 'never before seen Gospels' and late night TV documentaries will sometimes purport to uncover the 'real origins' of Christianity, none of this is likely to trouble informed Christians. When confronted by such media claims many modern believers will respond by asking for the actual argument or evidence thought to challenge their beliefs. Christianity has been around far too long and has been assessed by far too many critics to make the average intelligent Christian overly concerned about rumours of 'new evidence'. This is not to say new evidence may not be found in the future – the historical nature of Christianity means that it must always remain open to this possibility. My point is simply that Christian confidence is more solidly grounded than many outside the church (and outside scholarship) often realize.

To Christians reading this I would like to add a caveat. By all means, take the front foot in matters of the historical basis of Christ, but do so humbly and graciously. As the New Testament itself urges: 'Always be prepared to give an answer to everyone who asks you to give the reason for the hope that you have. But do this with gentleness and respect' (1 Peter 3:15). Christian faith is well grounded but it is not provable in a mathematical sense and it does not allow smugness. Modern believers should never treat sceptics with disdain for choosing not to accept the claims about Christ.

3. *Reading Jesus seriously*. I hope you will not mind my adding a personal challenge that arises from this discussion. I would love to think that this book will help you explore the Gospels with the same mental discipline you would give to important documents from your own favourite field – law, sport, medicine, carpentry, finance, retailing, education, language or whatever. I am not saying we need to become experts, or that Bible reading should be arduous. I am simply saying that readers of the Gospels can and should apply themselves to understanding the man from Nazareth with the same seriousness and attention to detail they would give to any other crucially important aspect of professional or personal life.

A selection of readings from ancient non-Christian sources

Mara bar Serapion (Syriac Manuscript Additional 14,658)

What advantage did the Athenians gain by murdering Socrates, for which they were repaid with famine and pestilence? Or the people of Samos by the burning of Pythagoras, because their country was completely covered in sand in just one hour? What advantage did the Jews gain from executing their wise king? It was just after that that their kingdom was abolished… But Socrates did not die altogether; he lived on in the teaching of Plato, Pythagoras did not die altogether; he lived on in the statue of Hera. Nor did the wise king die altogether; he lived on in the teaching which he had given.

Cornelius Tacitus (*Annals* 15.44)

Christians derived their name from a man called Christ, who during the reign of Emperor Tiberius had been executed by sentence of the procurator Pontius Pilate. The deadly superstition, thus checked for the moment, broke out afresh not only in Judaea, the first source of the evil, but also in the City of Rome, where all things hideous and shameful from every part of the world meet and become popular.

Pliny the Younger (*Letters* 10.96)

The sum total of their guilt or error was no more than the following. They had met regularly before dawn on a determined day, and sung antiphonally (i.e. alternately by two groups) a hymn to Christ as to a god. They also took an oath not for any crime, but to keep from theft, robbery and adultery, and not to break any promise.

Flavius Josephus (*Jewish Antiquities* 18.63–64)

At this time there appeared Jesus, a wise man. For he was a doer of startling deeds, a teacher of people who received the truth with pleasure. And he gained a following both among many Jews and among many of Greek origin. He was perhaps the Messiah-Christ. And when Pilate, because of an accusation made by the leading men among us, condemned him to the cross, those who had loved him previously did not cease to do so. For they reported that he had appeared to them three days after his crucifixion and that he was alive. And up until this very day the tribe of Christians, named after him, has not died out.

Talmud (*baraitha Sanhedrin* 43a–b)

On the eve of Passover Jesus was hanged [i.e. on a cross]. For forty days before the execution took place, a herald went forth and cried, 'He is going forth to be stoned because he has practised sorcery and enticed and led Israel astray. Anyone who can say anything in his favour, let him come forward and plead on his behalf.' But since nothing was brought forward in his favour, he was hanged on the eve of Passover.

2 Teacher
His words and their impact

There are two very common, significant mistakes people make in thinking about the man Jesus. The first is made by the general public; the second by Christians, especially of the Protestant variety (of which I am one).

Mistaken Jesuses

Probably the most enduring image of Jesus in contemporary society is that of a *Teacher*. If he is thought of at all, he is viewed as the archetypal wise man, someone who left behind great words to follow, a kind of Gandhi-figure. This was brought home to me powerfully when I took part in a discussion about Jesus some years ago on Triple J radio. The last 20 minutes of the show was talkback. Callers were invited to ring in and tell us what they thought of Jesus. Every caller – and there must have been ten – was surprisingly favourable toward Jesus.

What the callers loved about Christ were his words – the way he critiqued religious authority, demanded pacifism and preached love and tolerance toward all classes of people. We could have been talking about Gandhi! None of the participants mentioned Jesus' healings or his claim to be the Messiah, God's Son; there was nothing about his death on the cross or his reported resurrection to life. Jesus the *Teacher* was the only thing on the table.

This is the first significant mistake people make in assessing Jesus: they so magnify his role as Teacher that they end up diminishing, or ignoring altogether, some of the most striking and indispensable features of the Jesus of history. The result is a truncated Jesus; a Jesus of my preference and imagination.

But equally flawed is the Christian (especially Protestant) overreaction to the general public's Teacher-Jesus. In seeking to affirm his climactic role as the Saviour who died and Lord who rose again, some in the modern church so downplay his role as Teacher that he becomes almost unrecognizable as the Jesus of the Gospels, the Jesus of history. The conviction that he is *more* than a teacher can lead to the assumption that he is hardly a teacher at all. The teachings recorded throughout the middle chapters of the Gospels come to be thought of as a mere precursor to the *real* ministry of Christ recorded in the final chapters.

Even at theological college we were frequently told that almost a quarter of each of the four Gospels is given over to describing Jesus' death and resurrection. Mark's Gospel, in particular, was described to us as a 'Passion narrative with extended introduction'. It was not until years later that it dawned on me: if 25 per cent of each Gospel is concerned with Jesus' death and resurrection, this means 75 per cent is concerned with his life and teaching (mathematical insights have never been my strength).

I would certainly want to affirm that Jesus' death and resurrection are presented in the earliest Christian sources as his crowning achievements, and I will have a lot more to say about these in Chapters 9 and 10. All I am saying at this point is that, although Jesus was *more* than a teacher, he nevertheless *was* a teacher. Historically speaking, Jesus' fame as a teacher is one of the most prevalent themes of the ancient sources.

Jesus as 'Teacher' outside the Gospels

Everywhere in our sources Jesus appears as a teacher of great influence. Even our non-Christian sources refer to his effect as a teacher – for good or ill.

Mara bar Serapion, a pagan father writing home to his son (around AD 70), compares Jesus to the great Greek philosophers

Socrates and Pythagoras whose teachings continue on in the world long after their deaths: 'Nor did the wise king (Jesus) die altogether; he lived on in the teaching which he had given'.[19] The first-century Jewish historian, Josephus, said a similar thing:

> *At this time there appeared Jesus, a wise man. For he was a doer of startling deeds, a teacher of people who received the truth with pleasure. And he gained a following both among many Jews and among many of Greek origin.*
> ***Jewish Antiquities 18.63***

Mara and Josephus offer a somewhat neutral description of Jesus as Teacher. The ancient Talmud, an exposition of Jewish law, puts things in thoroughly negative terms: 'Jesus of Nazareth enticed and led Israel astray.'[20] This of course is a way of saying that Jesus influenced the nation more than the elite would have liked.

Jesus as 'Teacher' in the Gospels

An even clearer portrait of Jesus the Teacher is seen throughout the Gospels. Several points deserve brief mention. Firstly, Jesus' ministry is often summarized in the Gospels as one of teaching. In the first stage of Jesus' ministry (about AD 28), throughout Galilee, we read:

> *Jesus went through all the towns and villages, teaching in their synagogues, preaching the good news of the kingdom.*
> ***Matthew 9:35***

In the second stage of his ministry (about AD 29), around Judea, we read:

> *Jesus then left that place and went into the region of Judea and across the Jordan. Again crowds of people came to him, and as was his custom, he taught them.*
> ***Mark 10:1***

And in the final stage of his ministry (AD 30), in Jerusalem itself, Jesus declares to his captors:

Am I leading a rebellion, that you have come out with swords and clubs to capture me? Every day I sat in the temple courts teaching, and you did not arrest me.
Matthew 26:55

People also routinely addressed Jesus by the title 'Teacher'. For example, in the midst of the storm recorded in Mark 4 we read:

Jesus was in the stern, sleeping on a cushion. The disciples woke him and said to him, 'Teacher, don't you care if we drown?'
Mark 4:38

Again, in his final week, around Jerusalem, Mark 13 tells us:

As he was leaving the temple, one of his disciples said to him, 'Look, Teacher! What massive stones! What magnificent buildings!'
Mark 13:1

I suspect a Christian who regularly referred to Jesus as the 'Teacher' might be viewed a bit strangely by others in church circles. For some reason, it is just not part of ecclesiastical vocabulary anymore. I sometimes feel I should reintroduce it and see how it goes. At this point, the general public's emphasis on Jesus as a teacher is not as far off the mark as it is sometimes assumed.

Jesus referred to himself as 'Teacher'. The point is forcefully made in Matthew 23:8–10, where Jesus says to a crowd of his followers:

But you are not to be called 'Rabbi,' for you have only one Master and you are all brothers. And do not call anyone on earth 'father' [in the religious sense, that is], for you have one Father, and he is in heaven. Nor are you to be called 'teacher', for you have one Teacher, the Christ.

As it turns out, the first Christians did go on to address certain church officials as 'teachers'.[21] But this was only after a significant re-definition of what the word meant. The teacher's role in early Christianity was to memorize and pass on Jesus' words and deeds. Teachers were not fountains of the collective wisdom of the rabbis; they were more like repositories, or memory banks, for the wisdom of the one true Teacher. As British scholar Professor James Dunn of the University of Durham explains:

> *Teachers, indeed, seem to have been the first regularly paid ministry within the earliest Christian movement. Why teachers? Why else than to serve as the congregation's repository of oral tradition [memorized accounts of Jesus]?… All who read these pages will have been bred into a society long accustomed to being able to rely on textbooks, encyclopaedias, and other reference works. But an ancient oral society had few if any such resources and had to rely instead on individuals whose role in their community was to function… as 'a walking reference library'.*[22]

In short, teachers in early Christianity viewed themselves as the 'walking reference libraries' of the one true Teacher, Jesus.

The challenge of Jesus' teaching

This emphasis in the Gospels on Jesus as the *one true* Teacher highlights the serious challenge he posed to the teachers of his day. He consistently set his teaching against the centuries-old traditions of the rabbis of Israel. And the crowds knew it. At the end of Jesus' famous 'Sermon on the Mount' recorded throughout Matthew Chapters 5–7 we are told:

> *When Jesus had finished saying these things, the crowds were amazed at his teaching, because he taught as one who had authority, and not as their teachers of the law.*
> ***Matthew 7:28–29***

This is a very revealing statement, historically speaking. Matthew is not simply saying that Jesus was rhetorically more effective than the 'teachers of the law'. His mention of 'authority' here is a reference to the *chain of authority* the rabbis of the first century were commissioned to preserve. Virtually all Jewish teaching in this period involved listing the memorized rulings of former teachers on various ethical and legal matters. The authority of any given 'teacher of the law' consisted in his ability to draw upon the vast body of collective rabbinic wisdom.

The most important of these rabbinic teachings were eventually compiled in the second holy book of Judaism, the Mishnah – still regarded as Scripture by Orthodox and Conservative Jews. The Mishnah, as I said in Chapter 1, records the sayings of over 150 famous rabbis (from 50 BC – AD 200) organizing them into 63 subcategories. My copy runs to 1100 pages. When Matthew's Gospel says here that Jesus 'taught as one who had authority, and not as their teachers of the law', he means that Jesus cut right across the usual chain of rabbinic authority. He rejected it as a man-made edifice that obscured rather than clarified the will of God.

The ancient Jewish topic of hand washing provides a good point of comparison between the teaching of Jesus and the teaching of his contemporaries. One section of the Mishnah is called *Yadayim* ('hands'). It is an eight-page summary of the correct way to wash one's hands before eating a meal. Ritual washing was an important part of ancient Judaism:

> *The hands are susceptible to [spiritual] uncleanness and are rendered clean up to the wrist. How so? If one poured the first water [of two compulsory cleansings] up to the wrist, and the second beyond the wrist and it went back to the hand – it is clean. If he poured out the first and the second pouring of water beyond the wrist and it went back to the hand, it is unclean. If he poured out the first water onto one hand, and was reminded and poured out the second water on to both hands, they are unclean. If he poured out the first water on to both hands and was reminded and poured out the second water on to one hand, his hand, which has been washed twice, it is clean. If he poured out water on to one hand and rubbed it on the other, it is unclean.*[23]

Jesus rejected many of these purity rules, describing them as man-made traditions that distorted the wishes of the Almighty. In the Gospel of Mark we catch Jesus in full flight on the theme of *Yadayim*:

> *So the Pharisees and teachers of the law asked Jesus, 'Why don't your disciples live according to the tradition of the elders instead of eating their food with "unclean" hands?' He replied, 'Isaiah was right when he prophesied about you hypocrites; as it is written: "These people honour me with their lips, but their hearts are far from me. They worship me in vain; their teachings are but rules taught by men." You have let go of the commands of God and are holding on to the traditions of men.'*
> ***Mark 7:5–8***

For Jesus, what mattered was not the ethical artifice constructed by society – his or ours – but the direct will of God which he, as the one Teacher, claimed to embody.

Reflections

Part of the challenge of being a follower of Christ today is regularly pausing to separate out mere 'tradition' from the will of God revealed by the Teacher. Speaking personally, sometimes the process can be fun, as I realize that some of the things I have burdened myself with are just church culture. Other times, it can be disturbing as it dawns on me that some of what counts as 'normal' (in church or wider society) would be anathema to Jesus.

Following the Teacher will occasionally run counter to the world around us. It will at times be unpopular – a minority position. As Jesus warned in his Sermon on the Mount:

> *Enter through the narrow gate. For wide is the gate and broad is the road that leads to destruction, and many enter through it. But small is the gate and narrow the road that leads to life, and only a few find it.*
> ***Matthew 7:13–14***

Jesus probably intended this as a specific description of the response of first-century Israel to his teaching. But it has been disturbingly true of other periods as well. Sometimes – though not always – following Christ as Teacher is a lonely, counter-cultural experience. The wider public might like the *idea* of Jesus as Teacher but I am not sure it always has time for the actual *content* of his teaching. Some of what he said almost certainly puts aspects of Western culture (and church life) on the 'broad road' rather than the 'narrow' one.

Christians have often said that applying Jesus' teaching to everyday life at times feels like driving the wrong way up a one-way street (to extend Jesus' road metaphor). But this is to be expected if Jesus' claims are true and he really is the divinely appointed Teacher. A truth that is relevant for all human cultures will, by definition, contradict any particular human culture at some point, since societies are constantly in flux, sometimes coinciding with the truth, other times deviating from it.

People who seek to adjust Jesus' teaching – as the modern church sometimes does – in an attempt to make it more 'relevant' often end up doing just the opposite. In the first century as much as the twenty-first, the power and poignancy of Jesus' teaching is that it sounds like a voice from outside human society. It is a voice that knows us only too well, and it calls on us to live beyond the historical 'blip' of our particular culture.

So much more could be said but I want to close by pointing out the Gospels' counterpart to the theme of Jesus as Teacher: the Christian as 'disciple'. The word 'disciple', *mathētēs* in Greek, is the default term in the Gospels for a follower of Jesus – not just the so-called twelve apostles but all of his followers. It is used over 200 times. No other New Testament word for 'Christian' even comes close to this. 'Disciple' translates literally as *learner* or *pupil*. It is, as I said, the counterpart to Christ's role as *Teacher*.

The word 'disciple' reminds us that the historical Jesus wanted not just 'believers' who would pray and go to church but 'students' who would imbibe his words and seek to relate them to everyday life. If the selection of teachings quoted over the next few pages is anything to go by, I think we can safely conclude that the historical Jesus would want to ask the modern disciple a series of uncomfortable questions: Do you reflect on what I said about marriage and sex, and allow that to shape how you think and act in our sexually loaded society? Do you mull over what I said about clothes, food and the body (the obsessions of a pagan culture) and try to apply this to modern living? Do you ponder my teaching on poverty and wealth, and factor that into your household budget? Do you recall how I urged you to pray, and make that part of your routine? Do you contemplate my sayings on divine forgiveness, and soak them up for yourself and embody them toward others? Have you learnt what I meant by 'love your neighbour as yourself', and tried to express that in all of the radical ways I described?

A selection of readings from the teaching of Jesus

Christian character

Blessed are the poor in spirit, for theirs is the kingdom of heaven. Blessed are those who mourn, for they will be comforted. Blessed are the meek, for they will inherit the earth. Blessed are those who hunger and thirst for righteousness, for they will be filled. Blessed are the merciful, for they will be shown mercy. Blessed are the pure in heart, for they will see God. Blessed are the peacemakers, for they will be called sons of God. Blessed are those who are persecuted because of righteousness, for theirs is the kingdom of heaven.
Matthew 5:3–10

Sex and marriage

You have heard that it was said, 'Do not commit adultery.' But I tell you that anyone who looks at a woman lustfully has already committed adultery with her in his heart. If your right eye causes you to sin, gouge it out and throw it away. It is better for you to lose one part of your body than for your whole body to be thrown

into hell. And if your right hand causes you to sin, cut it off and throw it away. It is better for you to lose one part of your body than for your whole body to go into hell.
Matthew 5:27–30

How to pray

And when you pray, do not be like the hypocrites, for they love to pray standing in the synagogues and on the street corners to be seen by men. I tell you the truth, they have received their reward in full. But when you pray, go into your room, close the door and pray to your Father, who is unseen. Then your Father, who sees what is done in secret, will reward you. And when you pray, do not keep on babbling like pagans, for they think they will be heard because of their many words. Do not be like them, for your Father knows what you need before you ask him. This, then, is how you should pray: 'Our Father in heaven, hallowed be your name, your kingdom come, your will be done on earth as it is in heaven. Give us today our daily bread. Forgive us our debts, as we also have forgiven our debtors. And lead us not into temptation, but deliver us from the evil one.'
Matthew 6:5–13

Wealth, food and the body

No one can serve two masters. Either he will hate the one and love the other, or he will be devoted to the one and despise the other. You cannot serve both God and Money. Therefore I tell you, do not worry about your life, what you will eat or drink; or about your body, what you will wear. Is not life more important than food, and the body more important than clothes? Look at the birds of the air; they do not sow or reap or store away in barns, and yet your heavenly Father feeds them. Are you not much more valuable than they? Who of you by worrying can add a single hour to his life? And why do you worry about clothes? See how the lilies of the field grow. They do not labour or spin. Yet I tell you that not even Solomon in all his splendour was dressed like one of these. If that is how God clothes the grass of the field, which is here today and

tomorrow is thrown into the fire, will he not much more clothe you, O you of little faith? So do not worry, saying, 'What shall we eat?' or 'What shall we drink?' or 'What shall we wear?' For the pagans run after all these things, and your heavenly Father knows that you need them. But seek first his kingdom and his righteousness, and all these things will be given to you as well. Therefore do not worry about tomorrow, for tomorrow will worry about itself. Each day has enough trouble of its own.
Matthew 6:24–34

Caring for those in need

On one occasion an expert in the Law stood up to test Jesus. 'Teacher,' he asked, 'what must I do to inherit eternal life?' 'What is written in the Law?' he replied, 'How do you read it?' He answered: 'Love the Lord your God with all your heart and with all your soul and with all your strength and with all your mind'; and, 'Love your neighbour as yourself'. 'You have answered correctly,' Jesus replied. 'Do this and you will live.' But he wanted to justify himself, so he asked Jesus, 'And who is my neighbour?' In reply Jesus said: 'A man was going down from Jerusalem to Jericho, when he fell into the hands of robbers. They stripped him of his clothes, beat him and went away, leaving him half dead. A priest happened to be going down the same road, and when he saw the man, he passed by on the other side. So too, a Levite, when he came to the place and saw him, passed by on the other side. But a Samaritan, as he travelled, came where the man was; and when he saw him, he took pity on him. He went to him and bandaged his wounds, pouring on oil and wine. Then he put the man on his own donkey, took him to an inn and took care of him. The next day he took out two silver coins and gave them to the innkeeper. "Look after him," he said, "and when I return, I will reimburse you for any extra expense you may have." Which of these three do you think was a neighbour to the man who fell into the hands of robbers?' The expert in the law replied, 'The one who had mercy on him.' Jesus told him, 'Go and do likewise.'
Luke 10:25–37

Love for enemies

But I tell you who hear me: Love your enemies, do good to those who hate you, bless those who curse you, pray for those who mistreat you. If someone strikes you on one cheek, turn to him the other also. If someone takes your cloak, do not stop him from taking your tunic. Give to everyone who asks you, and if anyone takes what belongs to you, do not demand it back. Do to others as you would have them do to you. If you love those who love you, what credit is that to you? Even 'sinners' love those who love them. And if you do good to those who are good to you, what credit is that to you? Even 'sinners' do that. And if you lend to those from whom you expect repayment, what credit is that to you? Even 'sinners' lend to 'sinners', expecting to be repaid in full. But love your enemies, do good to them, and lend to them without expecting to get anything back. Then your reward will be great, and you will be sons of the Most High, because he is kind to the ungrateful and wicked. Be merciful, just as your Father is merciful.
Luke 6:27–36

Divine mercy

Suppose one of you has a hundred sheep and loses one of them. Does he not leave the ninety-nine in the open country and go after the lost sheep until he finds it? And when he finds it, he joyfully puts it on his shoulders and goes home. Then he calls his friends and neighbours together and says, 'Rejoice with me; I have found my lost sheep.' I tell you that in the same way there will be more rejoicing in heaven over one sinner who repents than over ninety-nine righteous persons who do not need to repent. Or suppose a woman has ten silver coins and loses one. Does she not light a lamp, sweep the house and search carefully until she finds it? And when she finds it, she calls her friends and neighbours together and says, 'Rejoice with me; I have found my lost coin.' In the same way, I tell you, there is rejoicing in the presence of the angels of God over one sinner who repents.
Luke 15:4–10

3 Healer
The deeds that baffle

We arrive unavoidably at an aspect of Jesus' ministry that for some is a source of awkwardness. In our scientifically informed culture, talk of the blind receiving sight, the dead being raised and storms being calmed seems like the baggage of an ignorant, superstitious past. Jesus the *Teacher* we can appreciate, but Jesus the *Healer*, miracle-worker: that is a little less digestible. Nevertheless, no historical treatment of Christ can sidestep this major aspect of the early portraits of the man.

In the following chapter I do not intend or even believe it possible to *prove* Jesus performed miracles. What I want to do, instead, is offer some philosophical and historical observations about miracles before turning to explore what the Gospels say is the *meaning* of Jesus' supposed startling deeds.

Philosophical observations about 'miracles'

The modern philosophical debate about miracles, which has been going on since the eighteenth century, has resulted in a stalemate – not a draw or a friendly handshake, but a begrudging realization that neither side has been able to deal the decisive blow.

Philosophically, the rationality (or otherwise) of a belief in miracles boils down to our prior assumptions about the world. If I assume that the observable laws of nature are the *only* forces active in the universe, then the fact that I do not observe miracles today will be interpreted quite reasonably as proof that miracles have never been observed, indeed, have never occurred.

No amount of evidence will be considered strong enough to convince me of the 'supernatural' nature of an event. I will always opt for a natural explanation no matter how complex that explanation must be. My assumption demands it.

If, on the other hand, I assume that the observable laws of nature are *not* the only forces active in the universe – that there is behind these laws a Law-Giver – then the fact that I personally do not observe miracles today will not be regarded as proof that miracles have never occurred. It may inspire a certain scepticism about miraculous claims but my assumption about a Law-Giver (God) gives me the freedom to accept a 'miraculous' interpretation of an event *if* the evidence points strongly enough in that direction.[24]

Put simply, openness to miracles is irrational if I hold the first assumption and rational if I hold the second. Hence, the debate about miracles often moves on to a debate over naturalism (the affirmation that physical forces are the only forces in the universe) versus theism (the affirmation that a Creative Mind stands behind the universe). And in philosophy there is something of a stalemate there too. This is not the book to unravel these mysteries. I simply want to underline that belief in miracles is not a historical question, as such; it is a philosophical one.

Turning from philosophy to history, let me make a few brief observations.

The absence of miracle workers in Jesus' world

Firstly, let me say something about historical reports of miracles in Palestine in the centuries either side of Jesus. It is sometimes said that miracle-workers were commonplace in Jesus' day and that the Gospels should be read in light of that wider trend in the ancient world: everyone was doing miracles, so the Gospel writers portrayed Jesus as doing the same! This is not quite accurate.[25]

While Jewish *exorcists* (those who cast out demons) appear to have been common, there are only two historical figures other than Jesus associated with healing miracles in this period. The first was Honi the Circledrawer who, in the century before Jesus, is reported to have prayed to God for rain during a drought. He stood inside a circle drawn on the ground and waited until God answered the prayer, which he reportedly did. The story is mentioned a century later by the historian Josephus and a century after that in the Mishnah.[26]

The second figure is Hanina ben Dosa who lived in Galilee a generation after Jesus. According to a source written a few centuries later, Hanina prayed for the desperately ill son of the famous Jerusalem rabbi, Gamaliel, and the boy dramatically recovered.[27]

From the historical perspective, it is difficult to know what to conclude about such isolated stories recorded a hundred or more years after the event in just one or two sources. My point, however, is that, even if these are reliable historical remembrances (and I incline to that conclusion), the parallel with Jesus is minimal if not non-existent. Honi and Hanina were not miracle-workers at all. They were simply pious Jews with a reputation for getting their prayers answered.

What we have in the Gospels is another thing entirely. Not only is the sheer number of Jesus' reported miracles striking (38 by scholarly count); so is the fact that they are said to occur through his *own* power. He restores a leper with a touch, a crippled man with a word, a dead girl with a command, a haemorrhaging woman by her contact with his robe, a demon-crazed man with a simple rebuke, and so on. Frankly, we have no historical accounts comparable to this in antiquity. Whatever else the Gospel reports are, they are not part of an ancient trend.

Jesus' healings in the historical sources

The startling deeds of Jesus are attested in multiple independent sources in both Christian and non-Christian writings from antiquity. On the Christian side, Mark, Q, Special L, Special M and the Signs Source all affirm Jesus' miraculous abilities.[28] To repeat what I said in Chapter 1, these 'Christian' sources are treated by historians as independent witnesses since, although they now appear together in our New Testament, they were originally separate traditions. Something other than collusion, in other words, gave rise to the consistent portrayal of Jesus as a miracle-worker.

From the Jewish and Greco-Roman sources we have at least two references to Jesus' miraculous activity. The first-century Jewish historian Josephus wrote: 'At this time there appeared Jesus, a wise man. For he was a doer of startling deeds…'[29] The word translated 'startling' here is the Greek term *paradoxos*, from which we get 'paradox'. It is a neutral, non-committal way of referring to Christ's inexplicable abilities.

Not so neutral is the legal judgment of the Jewish Talmud: 'On the eve of Passover Jesus was hanged (i.e. on a cross)… because he has practised sorcery and enticed and led Israel astray.'[30] What is fascinating is that among Jesus' opponents there was never any attempt to deny Jesus' strange abilities, only to cast them in a negative light, as involving 'sorcery' or the power of demons.

What modern historians say about Jesus' 'miracles'

It is because Jesus' 'startling deeds' are so widely and independently attested in ancient writings that most modern experts (whatever their religious persuasion) arrive at a similar conclusion: *Jesus did things that were interpreted by everyone around him as supernatural.* The wording of this statement is important. Historians cannot affirm (or deny) that Jesus actually did miracles – that would be to go beyond historical method to philosophical interpretation. What historians can (and do) affirm is that Jesus' friends and foes alike all conceded the supernatural nature of his ministry. This is a conclusion reached by virtually all of the leading scholars in the field: Graham Stanton of Cambridge University, James Dunn of the University of Durham, Martin Hengel of the University of Tübingen, Ed Sanders of Duke University, Richard Horsley of the University of Massachusetts and John Dominic Crossan of DePaul University.

Currently, the most voluminous modern scholar of the

historical Jesus is Professor John P. Meier of the University of Notre Dame in the United States. His magnum opus is the three-volume *A Marginal Jew: rethinking the historical Jesus*. Five hundred pages of volume two are given over to a rather exacting analysis of the historical data concerning Jesus' miracles. Keeping in mind that Meier happily rejects all sorts of other details in the Gospels, listen to his sober conclusion about the miracles:

> *The miracle traditions about Jesus' public ministry are already so widely attested in various sources and literary forms by the end of the first Christian generation that total fabrication by the early church is, practically speaking, impossible... Put dramatically but with not too much exaggeration: if the miracle tradition from Jesus' public ministry were to be rejected in toto as unhistorical, so should every other Gospel tradition about him. For if the criteria of historicity do not work in the case of the miracle tradition, where multiple attestation is so massive and coherence so impressive, there is no reason to expect them to work elsewhere. The quest would simply have to be abandoned. Needless to say, that is not the conclusion we have reached here.*[31]

That is where historical analysis of the question of Jesus' miracles leads us. That is also where it leaves us. How I go on from here to interpret this historical conclusion involves, as I have said, those prior assumptions. If I assume there are no forces in the universe other than the observable laws of nature, then I will feel well justified in searching for a natural interpretation of the data. If, on the other hand, I assume there is a Law-Giver behind the laws of nature, then, given the direction in which the historical evidence points, I will feel well justified in accepting a theological interpretation, such as that affirmed in the Gospels – to which I now want to turn.

Undoing Israel's curse

Rather than expound the Gospel text, I am trying to give readers some tools for reading the Gospels in a plausible historical framework. I want to provide a kind of 'Brodie's Notes' on Jesus, a summary, although I hope readers will study the set text as well.

What then is the significance of Jesus' miracles, from the point of view of the first-century Gospels? In addition to displaying Christ's power and compassion, the miracles have at least two important theological dimensions. The first has to do with ancient Israel specifically; the second has to do with the entire creation.

At the heart of the Jewish faith (the faith which Jesus shared) was a 'covenant', or agreement, between God and Israel made 1300 years before Christ. God promised to bless Israel as long as the nation reciprocated with worship of the Creator and justice toward other creatures. If Israel refused the path of worship and justice – so this covenant declared – the nation would experience a host of agreed-upon, nationwide disasters. In the fifth book of the Old Testament (what Jews call the Tanakh) Moses outlined some of the unhappy covenant curses:

> *However, if you do not obey the Lord your God and do not carefully follow all his commands and decrees I am giving you today, all these curses will come upon you and overtake you... The Lord will strike you with wasting disease, with fever and inflammation... The Lord will cause you to be defeated before your enemies... The Lord will afflict you with the boils of Egypt and with tumours, festering sores and the itch, from which you cannot be cured. The Lord will afflict you with madness, blindness and confusion of mind.*
> ***Deuteronomy 28:15–28***

It is important to realize that many Jews in Jesus' day understood themselves to be living under precisely these curses, and justifiably so. According to the Old Testament, between the ninth and sixth centuries BC Israel did turn its back on its covenant with God. The nation courted pagan deities and mistreated the poor and marginalized. As a result (so the Jewish people affirmed), God let his chosen people be conquered by invaders beginning with the Assyrians in the eighth century BC, the Babylonians in the sixth century BC, the Greeks in the fourth to third centuries BC and climaxing with the Romans in the first century BC. Moreover, Israel's God allowed his nation to be plagued with all manner of diseases: fever, leprosy, blindness, and demon-crazed madness. The covenant curses had fallen upon them.

The only thing mitigating the Jews' despondency in this period was the presence in the same Scriptures – the Christian Old Testament – of prophecies stating that after a period of judgment Israel would again experience a time of healing and restoration. The prophet Isaiah in the eighth century declared:

> *Then will the eyes of the blind be opened and the ears of the deaf unstopped. Then will the lame leap like a deer, and the mute tongue shout for joy.*
> ***Isaiah 35:5–6***

Later in the same book, the prophet says this healing would come through the ministry of a mysterious 'Servant of the Lord'. The Servant would himself bear the punishment of Israel and so deliver his people from the covenant curses:

> *Surely he [the 'Servant of the Lord'] took up our infirmities and carried our sorrows, yet we considered him stricken by God, smitten by him, and afflicted. But he was pierced for our transgressions, he was crushed for our iniquities; the punishment that brought us peace was upon him, and by his wounds we are healed.*
> ***Isaiah 53:4–5***

It is precisely in this biblical context that the healings of Jesus may, in large part, be understood. Jesus' repeated healing of just the sorts of ailments mentioned in the Old Testament – fever, skin-disease, blindness, madness, lameness, and so on – were a sign to ancient Jews that the covenant curses were being lifted from Israel. This is exactly how the Gospel of Matthew interprets Jesus' ministry. At the end of his account of the healing of a leper and the healing of a lame man Matthew writes:

> *When Jesus came into Peter's house, he saw Peter's mother-in-law lying in bed with a fever. He touched her hand and the fever left her, and she got up and began to wait on him. When evening came, many who were demon-possessed were brought to him, and he drove out the spirits with a word and healed all the sick. This was to fulfil what was spoken through the prophet Isaiah [in the passage quoted above]: 'He took up our [i.e. Israel's] infirmities and carried our diseases.'*
> ***Matthew 8:14–17***

Three chapters later, Jesus explains his miracles in terms of the promises of Isaiah 35 quoted earlier:

> *When John [i.e. John the Baptist] heard in prison what Christ was doing, he sent his disciples to ask him, 'Are you the one who was to come [i.e. Israel's promised restorer], or should we expect someone else?' Jesus replied, 'Go back and report to John what you hear and see: The blind receive sight, the lame walk, those who have leprosy are cured, the deaf hear [phrases all taken from the prophet Isaiah].'*
> ***Matthew 11:2–5***

In short, Jesus' healing ministry constituted a profound theological statement to Israel that the covenant curses described in the Old Testament book of Deuteronomy and elsewhere were being lifted in the ministry of Christ. The old covenant, with its blessings and curses, was being annulled; God's new covenant (for all nations) was being enacted.

A foretaste of God's kingdom

There is a second, equally important, biblical understanding of the miracles of Jesus. Put simply, Jesus' deeds are portrayed in our texts as a sign *within history* of the restoration of all things at the end of history. Jesus' power over sickness, evil and nature itself are a preview, you might say, of God's coming kingdom. This is a point Jesus himself makes at the end of a dispute with the Pharisees (a strict sect of first-century Jews) in the Gospel of Matthew:

> *Then they brought him a demon-possessed man who was blind and mute, and Jesus healed him, so that he could both talk and see. All the people were astonished and said, 'Could this be the Son of David?' But when the Pharisees heard this, they said, 'It is only by Beelzebub, the prince of demons, that this fellow drives out demons.' Jesus knew their thoughts and said to them, 'Every kingdom divided against itself will be ruined, and every city or household divided against itself will not stand. If Satan drives out Satan, he is divided against himself. How then can his kingdom stand? And if I drive out demons by Beelzebub, by whom do your people drive them out? So then, they will be your judges. But if I drive out demons by the Spirit of God, then the kingdom of God has come upon you.'*
> ***Matthew 12:22–28***

For the Pharisees, Jesus' miracles indicated the presence of devilish sorcery ('It is only by Beelzebub, the prince of demons, that this fellow drives out demons'). The same point is reiterated in the Jewish text discussed earlier.[32] For Jesus, however, his healing work indicates the presence not of the 'prince of demons' but of God's kingdom. He insists, 'But if I drive out demons by the Spirit of God, then the kingdom of God has come upon you.'

Interestingly, Jesus usually described God's kingdom as a *future* reality, when all creation will be brought into conformity to the wise and loving purposes of the Creator. In the well-known Lord's Prayer, for instance, he taught his disciples to pray 'Your kingdom come,' a plea for the arrival of God's dominion over the world. In the passage just quoted, however, Jesus clearly describes that kingdom as *present* in his ministry of healing and exorcism: 'the kingdom of God *has come upon you*'. What was usually described by Jesus (and the rest of the biblical writers) as an ultimate future reality is glimpsed, he maintained, in his startling deeds.

According to Christian Scripture, only in the final kingdom of God will there be no more pain, death and discord. As the second last chapter of the New Testament envisions:

> *He [God] will wipe every tear from their eyes. There will be no more death or mourning or crying or pain, for the old order of things has passed away.*
> ***Revelation 21:4***

But what is merely promised in prophecy and vision here in the book of Revelation (and elsewhere) was temporarily experienced within history, say the Gospels, in the ministry of Jesus: evil was overthrown, frail bodies were restored, nature itself was put right. The 'kingdom of God' had in *miniature* come upon them. And, as we have seen, it left its mark throughout our ancient sources. As much as the miracles point to Jesus' compassion and authority, fundamentally, they preview the renewal of all things in the kingdom to which Jesus invited his hearers.

Reflections

1. *Miracles today?* Firstly, for Christian believers in my readership I should probably add that I do believe that God in his mercy chooses to heal people today – sometimes through prayers, sometimes without them. He did this in Old Testament times; he will do it in contemporary times, the New Testament assures us (see for example James 5:14–16).

However, I want to stress this is not what the Gospels are trying to teach us in their accounts of Jesus' miracles (nor is it a point I wish to stress in this book). What Jesus did within history was not a program that can be enacted in the ongoing life of the church; it is rather a window into a future reality that is hoped for and proclaimed by the church.

2. *Restless hope*. The purpose of Jesus' startling deeds is not, within the logic of the Gospels, to evoke a belief in miracles today but rather to inspire a longing for the day when God's

kingdom comes fully upon the world. Throughout history, Christian faith has always involved a restless hope – a hope captured perfectly in the prayer 'Your kingdom come'. The previews of that kingdom which the miracles of Jesus provide have usually made Christ's followers dissatisfied with the way things are and desperate for the way things Christ said they would be. Christian hope is thus *confidently restless*: it praises God for the preview (in Jesus' life) and pleads for the finale (in the 'kingdom come'), when evil will be overthrown, humanity healed and creation itself renewed.

3. *A program for church and society*. Throughout the ages this restless hope has also inspired diligent work while we wait. Christians not only pray 'Your kingdom come'. They follow it with 'Your will be done on earth as it is in heaven.' In theory – and I will leave it to others to decide whether this is so in practice – those who have glimpsed the future in the healing deeds of Jesus commit themselves to serving the world, just as he did, in whatever way they can this side of the kingdom. They relieve suffering at every opportunity and resist evil wherever they see it. The creation of Christian hospitals and hospices in fourth-century Rome and the (largely Christian) movement to abolish slavery in eighteenth-century England were, in part, motivated by this ancient (theo)logic.

In *this* sense, Jesus' healing ministry recorded in the Gospels has provided a program for church and society. The logic is simple: while we do not yet possess all the resources of the 'kingdom come', we do know its aims – to renew human life and put an end to evil – and these are to shape what we strive for here and now.

A selection of readings from Jesus' startling deeds

Healing of a disabled man

A few days later, when Jesus again entered Capernaum, the people heard that he had come home. So many gathered that there was no

room left, not even outside the door, and he preached the word to them. Some men came, bringing to him a paralytic, carried by four of them. Since they could not get him to Jesus because of the crowd, they made an opening in the roof above Jesus and, after digging through it, lowered the mat the paralyzed man was lying on. When Jesus saw their faith, he said to the paralytic, 'Son, your sins are forgiven.' Now some teachers of the law were sitting there, thinking to themselves, 'Why does this fellow talk like that? He's blaspheming! Who can forgive sins but God alone?' Immediately Jesus knew in his spirit that this was what they were thinking in their hearts, and he said to them, 'Why are you thinking these things? Which is easier: to say to the paralytic, "Your sins are forgiven," or to say, "Get up, take your mat and walk"? But that you may know that the Son of Man has authority on earth to forgive sins'... He said to the paralytic, 'I tell you, get up, take your mat and go home.' He got up, took his mat and walked out in full view of them all. This amazed everyone and they praised God, saying, 'We have never seen anything like this!'
Mark 2:1–12

Healing of a leper and a servant

When he came down from the mountainside, large crowds followed him. A man with leprosy came and knelt before him and said, 'Lord, if you are willing, you can make me clean.' Jesus reached out his hand and touched the man. 'I am willing,' he said. 'Be clean!' Immediately he was cured of his leprosy. Then Jesus said to him, 'See that you don't tell anyone. But go, show yourself to the priest and offer the gift Moses commanded, as a testimony to them.'

When Jesus had entered Capernaum, a centurion came to him, asking for help. 'Lord,' he said, 'my servant lies at home paralyzed and in terrible suffering.' Jesus said to him, 'I will go and heal him.' The centurion replied, 'Lord, I do not deserve to have you come under my roof. But just say the word, and my servant will be healed. For I myself am a man under authority, with soldiers under me. I tell this one, "Go," and he goes; and that one, "Come," and he comes. I say to my servant, "Do this," and he does it." When Jesus heard this, he was astonished and said to those

following him, 'I tell you the truth, I have not found anyone in Israel with such great faith. I say to you that many will come from the east and the west, and will take their places at the feast with Abraham, Isaac and Jacob in the kingdom of heaven. But the subjects of the kingdom will be thrown outside, into the darkness, where there will be weeping and gnashing of teeth.' Then Jesus said to the centurion, 'Go! It will be done just as you believed it would.' And his servant was healed at that very hour.
Matthew 8:1–13

Turning water into wine

On the third day a wedding took place at Cana in Galilee. Jesus' mother was there, and Jesus and his disciples had also been invited to the wedding. When the wine was gone, Jesus' mother said to him, 'They have no more wine.' 'Dear woman, why do you involve me?' Jesus replied. 'My time has not yet come.' His mother said to the servants, 'Do whatever he tells you.' Nearby stood six stone water jars, the kind used by the Jews for ceremonial washing, each holding from twenty to thirty gallons. Jesus said to the servants, 'Fill the jars with water'; so they filled them to the brim. Then he told them, 'Now draw some out and take it to the master of the banquet.' They did so, and the master of the banquet tasted the water that had been turned into wine. He did not realize where it had come from, though the servants who had drawn the water knew. Then he called the bridegroom aside and said, 'Everyone brings out the choice wine first and then the cheaper wine after the guests have had too much to drink; but you have saved the best till now.' This, the first of his miraculous signs, Jesus performed at Cana in Galilee. He thus revealed his glory, and his disciples put their faith in him.
John 2:1–11

Healing of a bleeding woman and raising of a dead child

When Jesus had again crossed over by boat to the other side of the lake, a large crowd gathered round him while he was by the lake. Then one of the synagogue rulers, named Jairus, came there.

Seeing Jesus, he fell at his feet and pleaded earnestly with him, 'My little daughter is dying. Please come and put your hands on her so that she will be healed and live.' So Jesus went with him. A large crowd followed and pressed around him. And a woman was there who had been subject to bleeding for twelve years. She had suffered a great deal under the care of many doctors and had spent all she had, yet instead of getting better she grew worse. When she heard about Jesus, she came up behind him in the crowd and touched his cloak, because she thought, 'If I just touch his clothes, I will be healed.' Immediately her bleeding stopped and she felt in her body that she was freed from her suffering. At once Jesus realized that power had gone out from him. He turned around in the crowd and asked, 'Who touched my clothes?' 'You see the people crowding against you,' his disciples answered, 'and yet you can ask, "Who touched me?"' But Jesus kept looking around to see who had done it. Then the woman, knowing what had happened to her, came and fell at his feet and, trembling with fear, told him the whole truth. He said to her, 'Daughter, your faith has healed you. Go in peace and be freed from your suffering.'

While Jesus was still speaking, some men came from the house of Jairus, the synagogue ruler. 'Your daughter is dead,' they said. 'Why bother the teacher any more?' Ignoring what they said, Jesus told the synagogue ruler, 'Don't be afraid; just believe.' He did not let anyone follow him except Peter, James and John the brother of James. When they came to the home of the synagogue ruler, Jesus saw a commotion, with people crying and wailing loudly. He went in and said to them, 'Why all this commotion and wailing? The child is not dead but asleep.' But they laughed at him. After he put them all out, he took the child's father and mother and the disciples who were with him, and went in where the child was. He took her by the hand and said to her, 'Talitha koum!' (which means, 'Little girl, I say to you, get up!'). Immediately the girl stood up and walked around (she was twelve years old). At this they were completely astonished. He gave strict orders not to let anyone know about this, and told them to give her something to eat.

Mark 5:21–43

4 Israel
A nation on his shoulders

Coming in half way through a conversation

Have you ever come in half way through a conversation and completely misunderstood what people were talking about? Perhaps you came in just as your wife was criticizing her good-for-nothing husband, only to realize a moment later she was actually describing Homer Simpson in an episode from the cartoon series. Or perhaps you wandered past a good friend as he was mouthing off about 'Aborigines' and denigrating 'so-called refugees' only to discover with some relief that he was actually relating the right-wing views he had heard on the radio.

Sometimes, studying the life of Christ is like dropping in half way through a conversation. You read an account in the Gospels and you are not quite sure what it is all about. It seems there is some historical detail you are missing or some Old Testament background the Gospel writers expect you to know. Having this background illuminates the entire conversation and offers new insights into well-known but little understood aspects of Jesus' life or teaching.

In this chapter I want to explore an important claim in the Gospels that assumes you have been in on the conversation for a while. That conversation started back in the Old Testament, the Scriptures of ancient Israel. Once this aspect of Christ's life is set within that centuries-old conversation, an obscure and often overlooked part of the Jesus narrative brims with significance, both historical and personal.

Before we turn to Christ himself let me bring readers up to speed on the 'conversation' the Gospel writers assume you have been part of: the biblical story of Israel.

A spectator's guide to ancient Israel

Despite some occasional bad press, the Old Testament really tells a very straightforward narrative about God and his chosen nation, Israel. The story could be compared to an action-romance with more than a hint of tragedy: a noble prince rescues a slave girl, falls in love with her and marries her, only to have his heart broken by her unfaithfulness. That is the basic plot of the Jewish Scriptures. In fact, one of the Old Testament prophets uses a very similar analogy when recalling the history of God's people.[33]

The story of Israel begins sometime around 2000–1800 BC when, according to Genesis, the first book of the Old Testament, the Creator chose an idol-worshipping Mesopotamian named Abraham to be the patriarch of a brand new nation, one which would be divinely blessed and which would bring blessings to all the nations. Within a few generations, Abraham's descendants had grown into a sizable collective of twelve family clans, or tribes. These tribes were the direct descendants of the twelve sons of Jacob, the grandson of Abraham. Jacob's other name was 'Israel', which is why the twelve clans born to him came to be known collectively as Israel.[34]

Sadly for the chosen people, the next few hundred years were spent not in the land promised by God (the future 'land of Israel') but in Egypt where, under the famous Pharaoh Rameses II, they suffered the indignities of a slave nation set to work on the massive building programs of northern Egypt in the 1200s BC. God's people would not be oppressed for long, however. Under the leadership of Moses the Israelites found deliverance, an 'exodus' from slavery. The second book of the Old Testament, which is called Exodus, describes a series of divine disasters inflicted upon the tyrannous Egyptians resulting in the Pharaoh's decision to release the Israelites from slavery. In an event celebrated to this day in the Jewish

Passover festival, God rescued his people out of their distress and started them on their journey toward the Promised Land.

If the story so far can be likened to a prince rescuing his beloved, the next part of Israel's history reads like the marriage. A couple of months after the exodus from Egypt, God called Moses to go up a mountain somewhere in the Sinai Peninsula where he received an entire national constitution, known to Jews as the Torah. These laws would guide the newly liberated people of God as they settled in the land of Israel – the famous Ten Commandments were part of this constitution. The account of these laws – God's 'marriage contract' with Israel, we might say – fills the bulk of the next few biblical books (Exodus, Leviticus, Numbers and Deuteronomy).

The marriage, however, got off to a shaky start. No sooner had the nation agreed to live by this divine charter than they began to betray their rescuer in a host of ways. Between exiting Egypt and entering the Promised Land the twelve tribes lived as nomads in the deserts south and east of their future home. This 40-year period in Israel's history is known as the Wanderings – a description of both the geographical and moral realities of the time. There were some spectacular national 'sins' during the desert wanderings, including making and worshipping a golden calf,[35] constant grumbling against God and Moses[36] and a mass pagan orgy of Israelite men with Moabite women.[37] Many such incidents are related in the brutally honest books of Exodus and Numbers.

I wish I could say that God and Israel were soon reconciled and lived happily ever after. Instead these desert wanderings contain in miniature the basic plot of the whole Old Testament narrative. While the twelve tribes of Israel do eventually enter the Promised Land (1200 BC) and set up a successful monarchy and military machine (1000 BC), the spiritual story told alongside this political account makes for depressing reading.[38] Israel oppressed the poor, worshipped pagan deities and, despite the efforts of the Jewish prophets (750 BC – 600 BC), God's people refused to heed the call for reform. The Old Testament ends with Israel exiled from its own land at the hands of the invading

Babylonians (586 BC), leaving us wondering whether the Almighty's patience has run out.[39] The Old Testament prophets not only warned of destruction, they predicted a time of restoration for the twelve tribes of Israel, and not just for Israel but for the whole world.[40] This is where the New Testament picks up the story.

This potted history of biblical Israel sets the scene for the Gospels' portrait of Jesus. It is the first part of the conversation the Gospel writers invite us to join. To state things simply, but not inaccurately, the Gospels portray Jesus as the *new Israel*. In him, say these ancient sources, the entire story of God's people was being re-enacted, fulfilled, pardoned and rewritten.

Jesus as Israel called out of Egypt

Matthew's Gospel flags this theme as early as his second chapter. According to Matthew, Jesus' family avoided the wrath of King Herod by fleeing to Egypt – where there was a large Jewish community at the time. What is striking is that Jesus' return from Egypt, still as an infant, back to the land of Israel is described by Matthew as the fulfilment of an Old Testament statement specifically about the nation of Israel. Here is the passage:

> *So [Joseph] got up, took the child and his mother during the night and left for Egypt, where he stayed until the death of Herod. And so was fulfilled what the Lord had said through the prophet: 'Out of Egypt I called my son.'... After Herod died... [Joseph] got up, took the child and his mother and went to the land of Israel.*
> ***Matthew 2:14–21***

The prophetic words quoted by Matthew, 'Out of Egypt I called my son,' come from the Old Testament book of Hosea, chapter 11 verse 1. Everyone in Matthew's readership, however, knew that this statement was actually a reference to the liberation of Israel from Egyptian slavery back in the thirteenth century BC. Here is the quotation in its original context:

> *When Israel was a child, I loved him, and out of Egypt I called my son. But the more I called Israel, the further they went from me.*
> ***Hosea 11:1–2***

Hosea, writing in the eighth century BC, is lamenting the fact that, although God had rescued Israel from Egyptian slavery, the nation repaid him by refusing to follow his ways. As we have seen, this happened pretty much straight away. No sooner had they received God's laws (Torah), than they invented ways of breaking them during the 40 years of desert wanderings.

Matthew takes Hosea's statement about ancient Israel, God's national son, and applies it to Jesus, God's actual son. Just like Israel, Matthew says, Jesus was 'called out of Egypt' and led back to the promised land. Attentive first-century readers will have begun to scratch their heads trying to work out in what way Jesus might mirror ancient Israel. In particular, they will have wondered if this new 'son' would, like ancient Israel, refuse to heed the call of the Father. A few chapters later Matthew provides an answer to that question.

Jesus as Israel in the desert

One of the strangest incidents in Christ's life is recorded in different forms in three of the four Gospels (Matthew, Mark and Luke). Matthew's and Luke's reports of the episode are very similar and, in the opinion of most scholars, their accounts derive from their earlier shared source (known as Q). According to the passage, before Jesus embarked on his public career as a teacher and healer, he underwent a gruelling 40-day wandering through the deserts of southern Palestine.

At one level, a desert sojourn is not a surprising event. Other holy men of the period are known to have been active in the desert.[41] What is striking is that Jesus chose to wander the wilderness for *exactly* 40 days. Moreover, the temptations he faced during this period bear an uncanny resemblance to those faced by Israel in the famous 40-year wanderings described in the Old Testament books of Exodus, Numbers and Deuteronomy.

Keep in mind that the 'temptations' described in the following passage are probably to be thought of as a visionary experience at the climax of a 40-day fast. I shall quote the text from Matthew, then draw out some of the Old Testament connections:

> *Then Jesus was led by the Spirit into the desert to be tempted by the devil. After fasting forty days and forty nights, he was hungry. The tempter came to him and said, 'If you are the Son of God, tell these stones to become bread.' Jesus answered, 'It is written: "Man does not live on bread alone, but on every word that comes from the mouth of God".'*
>
> *Then the devil took him to the holy city and had him stand on the highest point of the temple. 'If you are the Son of God,' he said, 'throw yourself down. For it is written: "He will command his angels concerning you, and they will lift you up in their hands, so that you will not strike your foot against a stone".' Jesus answered him, 'It is also written: "Do not put the Lord your God to the test".'*
>
> *Again, the devil took him to a very high mountain and showed him all the kingdoms of the world and their splendour. 'All this I will give you,' he said, 'if you will bow down and worship me.' Jesus said to him, 'Away from me, Satan! For it is written: "Worship the Lord your God, and serve him only".' Then the devil left him, and angels came and attended him.*
>
> ***Matthew 4:1–11***

If we were not aware of the story of Israel described earlier, we might have glanced over this scene and missed its great significance for the Gospels' conversation about Jesus.

Jesus' 40-day desert trial appears to recall, indeed *re-enact*, Israel's 40-year desert trial a millennium or so before. The comparison is clear not just from the number '40' and the desert location, but especially from the fact that the temptations Jesus faced during this time are precisely those Israel faced during its wanderings. Moreover, all of the biblical quotations Jesus is said to have thrown back at the devil come straight out of the Old Testament account of Israel's 40 years in the desert. To anyone well versed in the ongoing conversation of Israel, Matthew 4 provides a powerful picture of someone re-enacting Israel's past and, by succeeding where Israel failed, rewriting the future. The details are intriguing, so I'll unpack them.

The first of Israel's three great temptations in the desert concerned food. The wandering nation grew sick and tired of eating 'manna from heaven' (divinely provided sustenance). They complained to Moses and arrogantly demanded that he arrange something more interesting for them: surely, if God could bend the might of Egypt, he could serve up a decent meal or two! Moses rebuked them for their ungrateful grumbling in words recorded in the Old Testament book of Deuteronomy:

> *Remember how the Lord your God led you all the way in the desert these forty years, to humble you and to test you in order to know what was in your heart, whether or not you would keep his commands. He humbled you, causing you to hunger and then feeding you with manna, which neither you nor your fathers had known, to teach you that man does not live on bread alone but on every word that comes from the mouth of the Lord.*
> ***Deuteronomy 8:2–3***

Notice that the closing words, 'man does not live on bread alone…', are exactly the words Jesus quotes when tempted to turn stones into bread to satisfy his hunger. Jesus prevails where Israel had succumbed.

Israel's second great sin in the 40-year desert wanderings was presuming to put the Lord to the test. At the slightest setback they demanded that God prove himself to them all over again, even though the deliverance from Egypt was still in living memory! Moses scolded them for this too. As the book of Deuteronomy records:

> *Do not test the Lord your God as you did at Massah [where they demanded fresh signs from God].*
> ***Deuteronomy 6:16***

When Jesus was urged to throw himself off the roof of the temple to test God's faithfulness to him, he quoted these very words of Moses in response. Again, Jesus proves faithful where Israel had proved faithless.

The third and most tragic of Israel's failures in the desert was, as I mentioned earlier, their worship of pagan deities. They made the mistake at least twice during the 40-year wanderings[42] and Moses pleaded with them:

> *Be careful that you do not forget the Lord, who brought you out of Egypt, out of the land of slavery. Fear the Lord your God, serve him only... Do not follow other gods, the gods of the peoples around you.*
> ***Deuteronomy 6:12–13***

Jesus quotes these very words when faced with a similar temptation. According to Matthew's Gospel, the devil took Jesus to a high mountain and 'showed him all the kingdoms of the world'. (Incidentally, I think this part of the narrative makes clear that we are meant to read these temptations as a *visionary* experience rather than as some kind of satanic teleportation: obviously, there is no vantage point from which one can view all the kingdoms of the world.) All of this could be yours, says the devil to Jesus, if only you worship me. Jesus does no such thing. Instead, he quotes Moses, remaining firm in his resolve to 'serve God only'. Yet again, where Israel had so tragically failed, Jesus – the new son of God – would prevail.

For Matthew's first readers this was evocative stuff. Every Jew knew that Israel's sins in the desert had been an ominous foreshadowing of the failures that would characterize the entire history of the nation. The desert sins were the beginning of the end for Israel's national and religious life. By submitting himself to a 40-day desert trial in which he would withstand the very temptations that had ruined Israel, Jesus was enacting a very powerful message for his Jewish brothers and sisters: in Christ, God's people can enjoy a new beginning, a rewriting of the tragic story of Israel. The call to follow Jesus, then, which we hear for the first time just a few paragraphs later in the Gospels,[43] is an invitation to break out of the previous story, with its cycle of sin and judgment, and enter into a new story – a new 'exodus' from slavery – and join a revived 'Israel', a new people of God.

Jesus and the twelve new tribes of Israel

According to all four Gospels, the call to follow Christ was first taken up by a small group of men whom Jesus designated 'apostles' (meaning 'sent ones'). The choice of these individuals was again informed by the ancient story of Israel. Let me quote the relevant passage and then explain what I mean:

> *Jesus went up on a mountainside and called to him those he wanted, and they came to him. He appointed twelve – designating them apostles – that they might be with him and that he might send them out to preach and to have authority to drive out demons. These are the twelve he appointed: Simon (to whom he gave the name Peter); James son of Zebedee and his brother John (to them he gave the name Boanerges, which means Sons of Thunder); Andrew, Philip, Bartholomew, Matthew, Thomas, James son of Alphaeus, Thaddaeus, Simon the Zealot and Judas Iscariot, who betrayed him.*
> ***Mark 3:13–19***

In light of the theme we have been exploring, it cannot be an accident that Jesus selected, and then commissioned, exactly *twelve* apostles. In the history of Israel the number twelve had a unique significance. You may remember it was the number of sons born to Abraham's grandson, Jacob (AKA 'Israel'); it was thus the number of tribes in the chosen nation. For Jews, 'twelve' always recalled the full complement of God's people.[44]

A saying of Jesus found in Matthew and Luke (deriving from their earlier source, Q) makes explicit this connection between the apostles and the twelve tribes of Israel. Jesus is here speaking about the future kingdom of God (discussed in the previous chapter) and the place of the apostles in it:

Peter answered him, 'We have left everything to follow you! What then will there be for us?' Jesus said to them, 'I tell you the truth, at the renewal of all things, when the Son of Man [i.e. Jesus] sits on his glorious throne, you who have followed me will also sit on twelve thrones, judging the twelve tribes of Israel.'
Matthew 19:27–28

All mainstream biblical historians affirm the fact and significance of Jesus' choice of twelve founding delegates. Professor Graham Stanton of the University of Cambridge sums up the scholarly consensus well:

What is the significance of the number twelve? Jesus' choice of this number provides an important clue to his intentions: the twelve were chosen by Jesus as the nucleus of the 'true' or 'restored' twelve tribes of Israel which he sought to establish... The importance of the call of the twelve can scarcely be exaggerated. In this prophetic action Jesus is calling for the renewal of Israel. He is also expressing the conviction that God is now beginning to establish anew his people – and will bring this promise to fulfilment.[45]

Jesus' miniature 'exodus' from Egypt and his re-enactment of Israel's 'desert wanderings' point in precisely the same direction as his selection of the twelve leaders of the budding Christian movement. Jesus was signalling to those around him that through his ministry God was re-writing the story of his people. The time of disobedience and judgment were over; the period of renewal had begun.

Reflections

Readers may be wondering whether such a historically specific aspect of Christ's life could have any relevance outside the context of first-century Israel. A few points are worth mentioning:

1. *Anti-Semitism*. I should clarify that Jesus' vision of the re-writing of Israel's story was not born out of anti-Semitism.

Jesus was a Jew, after all! He longed for the renewal of Israel, not its extinction. In the history of the Christian church this point has sometimes been too little appreciated. The portrayal of Jews as 'Christ-killers' whose place in God's affections was supplanted by the Church (a widespread Protestant viewpoint in sixteenth- to twentieth-century Europe[46]) has no basis in the New Testament.

The theological relationship between the Christian Church and the Jewish community is, frankly, a *mystery*: in fact, that is exactly the word Romans 11:25–32 uses of this relationship. But one thing is clear: for all his criticisms of his fellow Israelites, the historical Jesus was intent on inviting 'chosen people' to find in him all that their ancient Scriptures had promised.

2. *Jesus as the representative of God's people*. What is the relevance of all this for those *outside* of Jesus' first hearers? At this point I hope readers will permit me to do a bit of theology. According to the rest of the New Testament, Jesus (the ideal Israel) is the one who *represents* God's people before the Almighty himself. Here we arrive at a subtle but potent biblical theme, one Christians down through the ages have cherished. Jesus performed the obedience throughout his life that we in our frailty, like ancient Israel, could never fully offer.

According to the New Testament, Christ's obedience is the obedience God accepts *on behalf* of others. What he did – from his successful 40-day trial to his final breath – is counted as the faithfulness of all who follow him. He is our priest and representative. This is exactly how one book in the New Testament, aptly titled Hebrews, reflects upon the theme of Jesus' (desert) temptations. The passage is complex but the central point is clear:

> *Therefore, since we have a great high priest who has gone through the heavens, Jesus the Son of God, let us hold firmly to the faith we profess. For we do not have a high priest who is unable to sympathize with our weaknesses, but we have one who has been tempted in every way, just as we are – yet was without sin [probably a reference to the desert temptations]... Although he was a son, he*

learned obedience from what he suffered and, once made perfect, he became the source of eternal salvation for all who obey him and was designated by God to be high priest in the order of Melchizedek [an important Old Testament character]. We have much to say about this, but it is hard to explain because you are slow to learn.
Hebrews 4:14–5:11

I would not want to echo the sentiment of the final clause, but I would like to emphasize the writer's main point: Jesus' obedience (from his wilderness temptations to his death) is the full obedience none of us is able to offer the Creator. As the priest who represents us to God, his obedience is the 'source of salvation' for all who obey him, even though their obedience will only ever be a dim reflection of his.

As I was writing this chapter a friend expressed a common contemporary response to Christ's message: 'But sometimes it's so difficult,' she said. 'He set the bar so high, I don't know if I can do it.' At one level, this is an appropriate response to Christ's demands – his teaching discussed in Chapter 2 has deep implications for the whole of life. But it must be balanced, as I explained to my friend, with knowing that, according to the New Testament, Jesus' fully obedient life (and death) more than makes up for our frequently disobedient lives. As another New Testament writer put it:

But if anybody does sin, we have one who speaks to the Father in our defence – Jesus Christ, the Righteous One. He is the atoning sacrifice for our sins.
1 John 2:1–2

Put another way, believers live out their imperfect stories within the larger *perfect* story of the 'Righteous One'. Following him, however imperfectly, is perfect membership in God's new Israel.

3. *The model of obedience.* As long as we remember that our standing before God is dependent on Jesus' obedience, not our own, it is entirely appropriate to view the Christian life as

being fundamentally about trying to do what Jesus did – to be like him. The deeds we perform are not the means of writing ourselves into God's good books but they are the obvious consequence of knowing that we have been written into that book already.

Followers of Christ daily try to copy Jesus' story into their own life story. Like him, they try to resist the temptation to grumble at God's provision. They remind themselves that man does not live by bread (and BMWs) alone. Like him, they say no to putting God to the test by demanding signs from him, insisting that he do things their way, and so on. Like him, they refuse to bow down to the gods of their age – to the Dollar, the Body, the never-ending Renovation. They say with Jesus, 'Worship the Lord your God, and serve him only.'

As the new Israel, Jesus represents his people before God. As the new Israel, Jesus models what it means to live as the people of God. And the Christian life is lived out within these two realities.

5 Christ
More than a surname

Growing up I sincerely thought 'Christ' was a surname. After all, people used the words 'Jesus Christ' the way they might say 'Adam Gilchrist'. It seemed reasonable to me at the time that there would also have been a Mary and Joseph Christ, an Auntie Christ, a Grandpa Christ and so on down the Christ family tree. Little did I know that 'Christ' was a prestigious title. Even less did I know that it was a title of central importance to *two* world religions, not just one.

The 'Christ' of traditional Judaism

To this day, observant Jews pray earnestly for the ruler promised in their Scriptures (the Tanakh or Old Testament), descended from King David (1000 BC), who would liberate Israel from its enemies and establish the kingdom of God in the world. Each day of the week, Orthodox Jews recite words that have been part of Judaism since before the time of Jesus. The prayer, from the Siddur (or Jewish Prayer Book), pleads:

> *The offspring of Your servant David may You speedily cause to flourish, and enhance his glory through Your salvation, for we hope for Your salvation all day long.*
> ***Shemoneh Esrei 15***

Another prayer for this promised king appears (again in the Siddur) in the Jewish equivalent of a 'grace', said during meal times every mid-week day.

> *Have mercy, our God, on Israel Your people; on Jerusalem, Your city, on Zion, the resting place of Your Glory; on the monarchy of the house of David, Your Anointed.*
> ***Rahem, Third Blessing after Meals***

The all-important word here, 'Anointed', translates the Hebrew term *mashiah* (anglicized as 'Messiah'), which in Greek is *christos* (anglicized as 'Christ').

The idea of anointed kings or Messiahs or Christs goes right back to the time of the biblical prophet Samuel 1000 years before Jesus. The most significant of all of Samuel's duties was to commission, by 'anointing', a young shepherd boy named David (of David and Goliath fame):

> *The Lord said to Samuel, '... Fill your horn with oil and be on your way; I am sending you to Jesse of Bethlehem. I have chosen one of his sons to be king'... Then the Lord said, 'Rise and anoint him; he is the one.' So Samuel took the horn of oil and anointed David in the presence of his brothers, and from that day on the Spirit of the Lord came upon David in power.*
> ***1 Samuel 16:1–13***

King David was not the first or last person in the Bible to undergo an anointing ceremony, but he was considered the model of a king anointed with God's Spirit and power. He was, if you like, the first messiah, the first christ.

The central importance of David for the notion of an ultimate future Messiah–Christ was fixed forever in Jewish belief because of a prophecy given to King David by another prophet, Nathan, Samuel's successor. According to the prophecy, David's kingdom would somehow reign eternal:

> *When your days are over and you rest with your fathers, I will raise up your offspring to succeed you, who will come from your own body, and I will establish his kingdom... Your house and your kingdom will endure forever before me; your throne will be established forever.*
> ***2 Samuel 7:12–16***

It is impossible to overstate the importance of these words for both Judaism and Christianity. The hope for an eternal kingdom established by God, and administered by a descendant of King David, is at the heart of Jewish and Christian hope.

Even when David's 400-year historical dynasty collapsed in the sixth century BC, Jews clung to this ancient prophecy as their great hope. The prophets during this period of Israel's demise reiterated this ancient promise by insisting that out of the 'stump' of David's fallen family tree would emerge a Spirit-anointed king who would fulfil the hopes of Israel and govern the world forever. Consider this promise in the Old Testament book of Isaiah:

> *A shoot will come up from the stump of Jesse [Jesse was David's family name]; from his roots a Branch will bear fruit. The Spirit of the Lord will rest on him... He will not judge by what he sees with his eyes, or decide by what he hears with his ears; but with righteousness he will judge the needy, with justice he will give decisions for the poor of the earth. He will strike the earth with the rod of his mouth; with the breath of his lips he will slay the wicked... In that day the Root of Jesse will stand as a banner for the peoples; the nations will rally to him.*
> ***Isaiah 11:1–10***

This is the anointed king Jews long for daily in the words: 'Have mercy, our God... on the monarchy of the house of David, Your Anointed.' Please fulfil your promise, dear Lord, say Orthodox Jews each morning and at meal times; send us your Messiah–Christ, the banner for all nations.

The Christ of Christianity

Only when you understand this deep Jewish longing for the Davidic Messiah will you appreciate the enormity and scandal of the Gospels' emphatic claim that this *anointed one* is to be found in the Teacher and Healer from Nazareth. Matthew begins his Gospel with the words:

A record of the genealogy of Jesus Christ the son of David.
Matthew 1:1

The central paragraph of Mark's Gospel records:

'But what about you?' he [Jesus] asked. 'Who do you say I am?' Peter answered, 'You are the Christ.'
Mark 8:29

In Luke's Gospel, Jesus' trial revolves around this claim:

'We have found this man subverting our nation. He opposes payment of taxes to Caesar and claims to be Christ, a king.'
Luke 23:2

The summary at the end of John's Gospel states bluntly:

But these [things] are written that you may believe that Jesus is the Christ.
John 20:31

Historically speaking, more important than all of these quotations from the Gospels is the fact that our earliest Christian writings, the letters of the apostle Paul, refer to Jesus as 'Christ–Messiah' literally hundreds of times. What's more, many of these appear without the definite article: he is simply 'Christ' rather than '*the* Christ'. For the historian, this is significant. It indicates that as early as the 40s AD the title Christ–Messiah was so closely associated with Jesus that it was almost being used as his name, not just his title.[47]

It is no exaggeration to say that the central claim about Jesus in earliest Christianity was that he was the promised Christ–Messiah. More than a *Teacher* or *Healer* or the new *Israel*, Jesus was announced to all as the descendant of King David anointed by God to fulfil the hopes of Israel and to 'rally the nations' under his command, just as the ancient prophecy of Isaiah 11:10 quoted earlier had promised.

Interestingly, these claims were heard and reported by

non-Christian writers of the period as well. The Roman writers Suetonius and Tacitus refer to Jesus as 'Christ', even though they would have had little idea of what the title implied.[48] Even the first-century *Jewish* historian Josephus describes Jesus in words that apparently did not come easily off the pen:

> *He gained a following both among many Jews and among many of Greek origin. He was perhaps the Messiah–Christ.*
> **Josephus, *Jewish Antiquities* 18.63–64**

Later in his work, when he comes to narrate the martyrdom of Jesus' brother James, Josephus uses a similar awkward expression:

> *Ananus the high priest assembled the Sanhedrin of judges, and brought before them the brother of Jesus the so-called Messiah–Christ, whose name was James, and some others. When he had formed an accusation against them as breakers of the law, he delivered them over to be stoned to death.*[49]

Obviously, Josephus (a Jewish Pharisee) did not endorse Jesus as the Messiah. His words do, however, confirm that in the first century the principal claim about Jesus heard far and wide was that he was the Christ, God's anointed king over the nations.

Jesus and the messianic job description

But why, we may ask, were only tens of thousands of Jews convinced by Jesus' claims, instead of hundreds of thousands or even millions?[50] There are certainly socio-political factors we could talk about, but the principal reason probably lies in the fact that Jesus did not fit the job description expected of a Messiah in first-century Palestine. Remember the messianic prophecy of Isaiah:

> *He will not judge by what he sees with his eyes, or decide by what he hears with his ears; but with righteousness he will judge the*

> *needy, with justice he will give decisions for the poor of the earth. He will strike the earth with the rod of his mouth; with the breath of his lips he will slay the wicked… In that day the Root of Jesse will stand as a banner for the peoples; the nations will rally to him.*
> ***Isaiah 11:4–11***

In Jesus' day, this messianic language was interpreted in military terms. The 'needy' and 'poor' were of course the Jews; the 'wicked' were the Romans who ruled the Holy Land from 63 BC; and the Messiah's 'mouth' and 'breath' were his commands to slay Israel's enemies. The 'rallying' of the nations mentioned here was nothing less than the world's final submission to a Jewish king.

The alternative interpretation (offered by the followers of Jesus) was not widely considered: the 'needy' are all who need God; the 'wicked' are all who do injustice; the Messiah's 'mouth' and 'breath' are simply his world-conquering teaching; and the 'rallying' of the nations to him is the world's willing acceptance of him as history's true Lord. Given some hindsight, there can be little doubt that Jesus of Nazareth fits this second interpretation rather well. Within three centuries, the Roman Empire was indeed bowing the knee to the teaching of Christ. Today, Jesus is revered as Christ in more than 2000 languages among two billion people scattered across all 238 UN listed countries.[51]

Of course, hindsight is a beautiful thing. In the first century, worldwide devotion to a Jewish teacher was not what the Jews hoped for when they looked at their ancient prophecies. They longed for a military Messiah, one who would crush Israel's enemies by divine force. Evidence of this expectation is found not only in the numerous anti-Roman movements we know of among Jews of the period[52] but also in some of the pious texts composed at the time.

Around 50 BC, just a decade or so after Pompey's armies marched onto Israel's sacred soil, a Jewish leader in Jerusalem wrote a prayer pleading God to send a particular kind of Messiah. In short, he wanted a military commander descended from David who would smash the foreigners to pieces:

> *See, O Lord, and raise up for them [the Jewish people] their king, the son of David, to rule over your servant Israel in the time known to you, O God. Undergird him with the strength to destroy the unrighteous rulers [the Romans], to purge Jerusalem from gentiles who trample her to destruction; in wisdom and in righteousness to drive out the sinners from the inheritance; to smash the arrogance of sinners like a potter's jar. There will be no unrighteousness among them in his days, for all shall be holy, and their king shall be the Lord Messiah.*
> ***Pseudepigrapha, Psalms of Solomon 17.21–32***

Clearly, the 'Lord Messiah' described in this text is different from the figure we find in the pages of the Gospels. This Messiah would 'smash' the sinners; Jesus offered sinners forgiveness and transformation (as we shall see in Chapter 7). This Messiah would lead a successful rebellion against the foreign invaders; Jesus said 'love your enemies, do good to them' (Luke 6:35). Jesus did not fit any messianic job description we know of from the period, and some of his teachings ran completely counter to the little we do know about first-century aspirations.

This insight in part solves one of the puzzles in the Gospels. Scholars have often wondered why Jesus was so cagey about publicly accepting the title Messiah/Christ – frequently he even told people not to spread the word about him.[53] One explanation of this feature, made plausible in light of the above passage, is that Jesus did not want people to associate him with the kind of Messiah expected in Jerusalem at the time. Only when it was crystal clear that he had *not* come to 'destroy the unrighteous rulers' would he allow the title 'Messiah' to be connected with his ministry.

The people of the Messiah

In the central passage of Mark's Gospel, taken up by Luke and Matthew as well, Jesus describes what embracing *his* version of the Messiah will involve. To set the scene, it is perhaps half way through Jesus' three-year public career as a teacher and healer. He stops and asks his twelve apostles *who* they think they have been travelling with for the last 18 months or so. The episode is both a climax and an anti-climax:

> *'But what about you?' he asked. 'Who do you say I am?' Peter answered, 'You are the Christ.' Jesus warned them not to tell anyone about him. He then began to teach them that the Son of Man must suffer many things and be rejected by the elders, chief priests and teachers of the law, and that he must be killed and after three days rise again. He spoke plainly about this, and Peter took him aside and began to rebuke him. But when Jesus turned and looked at his disciples, he rebuked Peter. 'Get behind me, Satan!' he said. 'You do not have in mind the things of God, but the things of men.'*
>
> *Then he called the crowd to him along with his disciples and said: 'If anyone would come after me, he must deny himself and take up his cross and follow me. For whoever wants to save his life will lose it, but whoever loses his life for me and for the gospel will save it. What good is it for a man to gain the whole world, yet forfeit his soul? Or what can a man give in exchange for his soul? If anyone is ashamed of me and my words in this adulterous and sinful generation, the Son of Man will be ashamed of him when he comes in his Father's glory with the holy angels.'*
>
> ***Mark 8:29–38***

Here it is clear that Jesus' messianic mission is not to 'purge Jerusalem from gentiles', as the Jewish text quoted earlier suggested, but to suffer, die and rise again. With almost 2000 years of Christianization in the way it is difficult for modern readers to appreciate just how shocking this notion of a suffering Messiah would have been. We catch a glimpse of it in the response of the chief apostle, Peter, who took his master aside and 'rebuked him'. Jesus responds, so Mark's Gospel tells us, with his own stinging rebuke contrasting human ambitions for the Messiah with those of God: 'You do not have in mind the things of God,' he says to Peter, 'but the things of men.'

So great is Peter's misunderstanding of the Messiah's

mission that Jesus calls the crowd together in the second paragraph just quoted and makes clear that following him will not involve 'gaining the world'; instead, it means 'taking up a cross'. The contrast here is between two ways of being the people of the Messiah. The first tries to protect its interests and 'gain the world'. In historical context, this is not a reference to materialism but to messianic imperialism – the attempt to dominate the nations. Such a path, says Jesus, will result in the loss of one's soul before God.

The true way of belonging to the Messiah involves denying such ambitions and deciding to follow Jesus and his words wherever they lead – to loving one's enemies, doing good to one's persecutors, and even to a cross. The climactic words about being 'ashamed of me and my words in this adulterous and sinful generation' have little to do, then, with Christians feeling coy about their faith in a secular world. In its original setting they can only mean that following a crucified Messiah in a culture that wanted the Messiah to crucify the Romans would bring public shame. Disciples must be willing to bear this.

In short, Jesus appears to have demanded that people give up their private preferences and interpretations of what following the Messiah means, and entrust themselves to him utterly, wherever it leads. Being the people of the Messiah involves absolute, unconditional loyalty to the one whom God has anointed as the rallying point for the nations.

Reflections

A story is told – though I have not been able to verify it – of a young soldier in the army of Alexander the Great (356–323 BC). As Alexander moved east toward India and conditions became bitterly difficult, soldiers began to desert. Deserters were usually tracked down by a crack team of loyalists and executed. One such deserter, however, so the story goes, was captured by Alexander's men and brought before the king, in what must have been a terrifying experience for a young solider.

Alexander is said to have spared the deserter, but not before asking him his name. The soldier replied, 'I share the name of my king; I too am Alexander.' The king paused and replied in words that I can only imagine left a mark on the boy: 'Young man, you change your life or you change your name.'

In almost every respect Jesus was utterly different from the all-conquering Alexander. But there is logic to these words that Christians throughout the centuries have found compelling. Calling oneself a 'Christian' involves bearing the name of the greater king – the Christ. And that will change one's life. Private preferences and interpretations of what it means to follow Christ will be sacrificed. 'Crosses' will be taken up in readiness to follow him wherever it leads.

For the first few hundred years of Christian history, bearing this name was a risky business. A year or so after Jesus' death, a leader of the Greek-speaking disciples in Jerusalem, named Stephen, was put to death by stoning (AD 31/32).[54] In AD 42 the first of the twelve apostles, James son of Zebedee, was likewise martyred, this time by beheading.[55] After a period of relative calm, the 60s AD saw the killing of James the brother of Jesus (AD 62),[56] the apostles Peter and Paul (AD 64/65),[57] and scores of unnamed disciples whose dreadful fate under Nero's reign (AD 54–68) made even the Roman official Tacitus (AD 56–120) wince:

> *Nero substituted as culprits, and punished with the utmost refinements of cruelty, a class of men, loathed for their vices, whom the crowd styled Christians... First, then, the confessed members of the sect were arrested; next, on their disclosures, vast numbers were convicted ... And derision accompanied their end: they were covered with wild beasts' skins and torn to death by dogs; or they were fastened on crosses, and, when daylight failed were burned to serve as lamps by night. Nero had offered his Gardens for the spectacle, and gave an exhibition in his Circus, mixing with the crowd in the habit of a charioteer, or mounted on his car. Hence, in spite of a guilt which had earned the most exemplary punishment, there arose a sentiment of pity, due to the impression that they were being sacrificed not for the welfare of the state but to the ferocity of a single man [i.e. Nero].*
>
> **Tacitus, *Annals 15.44***

The words of Mark 8:34, 'If anyone would come after me, he must deny himself and take up his cross and follow me', must have had special resonance for the first followers of Jesus. They had watched their 'king' suffer and die, and now they were required to walk the same path.

It must have been tempting at times to take matters into their own hands – as, unfortunately, the church of a later time did – and seek to establish the Messiah's kingdom by force. But the early disciples knew, against all the currents of their society, that this was not the way of God and his Anointed One. Christians of this period bore the name (and the shame) of their king whatever the outcome.

The modern church would do well to remember this lesson when it too is tempted to establish itself in society by force (whether political or military). It would do well to heed the warning of the Messiah himself: 'What good is it for a man to gain the whole world, yet forfeit his soul?'[58]

6 Judge
His pledge to bring justice

Years ago, I was speaking to students in a high school in Sydney's southwest. I asked them to imagine their life – every deed, word and even thought – recorded on film and shown to family and friends. The awkwardness in the room was palpable. I then asked, 'What if God could see that film and decided to hold it against us?' One young man in the audience, unaware my wife would overhear him, mumbled to himself, 'I'd be stuffed.'

This is not the most theologically articulate response I have heard, but it is instinctively appropriate. The thought that the Almighty knows our every thought, word and deed, and that he has the right to hold us accountable, has caused most men and women over the millennia to reflect on their lives with seriousness and humility.

Nowadays, people usually object to any idea of God as wrathful. Part of the reason for this, I suspect, is revulsion at the 'fire and brimstone' preaching in some quarters of the church. An elderly friend of mine was put off church in her early thirties after hearing a series of very angry sermons about divine judgment. It seemed to Judy that the preacher quite enjoyed telling people of their impending doom. It was another three decades before she took another look at the faith of her youth.

There is of course another reason people recoil from the concept of God's judgment: we simply do not like it. Cognitive dissonance theory in psychology tells us that people tend to modify, or create, beliefs to suit their preferences. This is sometimes thrown at religious people in the form: 'You want a father figure in the sky, so you invent a god to believe in.' However, the boot is frequently on the other foot. The inconvenience of the notion of the Almighty, especially one who might be displeased with the way I live, is a powerful motivator to exclude such a 'god' from my thinking. It is not that such a god is inherently implausible or not in keeping with the facts; it simply does not suit my preference. The preferred God, for many in contemporary society, is the vague, distant Creator, the one who kicked off the universe and now, if he thinks of us at all, warmly approves of most of what we do.

This contemporary perspective makes it difficult for many today to approach objectively, it has to be said, what is an unavoidable part of the historical portrait of Jesus of Nazareth. He regularly taught about divine judgment and even cast himself as the agent of that judgment. Before we look at the data concerning Jesus, his teaching must be set within its biblical-historical context.

Divine judgment and love in the Bible

Repeatedly and without embarrassment the Bible declares that the true God is a God of justice as well as love. In biblical thought the idea of judgment in no way contradicts the reality of divine love. The two are often spoken about together. It is no exaggeration to say that throughout the Bible God's judgment is frequently portrayed as a consequence of his compassion.

According to the Old Testament book of Exodus, God's concern for the enslaved Israelites is what moved him to overthrow their brutal Egyptian overlords. The turning point in the narrative reads:

> *The Israelites groaned in their slavery and cried out, and their cry for help because of their slavery went up to God. God heard their groaning and he remembered his covenant with Abraham, with Isaac and with Jacob. So God looked on the Israelites and was concerned about them.*
> ***Exodus 2:23–25***

This was no simple divine favouritism, since no sooner had God's people left Egypt than he gave them instructions about their obligation to care for the downtrodden. If the Israelites oppressed the weak and poor, declared the Jewish Torah, they too would be overthrown:

> *Do not mistreat an alien or oppress him, for you were aliens in Egypt. Do not take advantage of a widow or an orphan. If you do and they cry out to me, I will certainly hear their cry. My anger will be aroused, and I will kill you with the sword; your wives will become widows and your children fatherless.*
> ***Exodus 22:21–24***

And five centuries later this is exactly what happened. The Assyrians ousted the Israelites 'with the sword' and, according to the prophet Ezekiel (among others), this was largely because Israel had oppressed the needy within its borders:

> *Her (Israel's) officials within her are like wolves tearing their prey; they shed blood and kill people to make unjust gain. Her prophets whitewash these deeds for them by false visions and lying divinations. They say, 'This is what the Sovereign Lord says' – when the Lord has not spoken. The people of the land practise extortion and commit robbery; they oppress the poor and needy and mistreat the alien, denying them justice. I looked for a man among them who would build up the wall and stand before me in the gap on behalf of the land so that I would not have to destroy it, but I found none. So I will pour out my wrath on them and consume them with my fiery anger, bringing down on their own heads all they have done, declares the Sovereign Lord.*
> ***Ezekiel 22:27–31***[59]

Not surprisingly, we observe the same connection between human injustice and divine judgment in the New Testament. For example, James the brother of Jesus insisted that God is so moved by the cries of the poor and defenceless that he will one day bring his wrath upon the rich oppressors of the world:

> *Now listen, you rich people, weep and wail because of the misery that is coming upon you. Your wealth has rotted, and moths have eaten your clothes. Your gold and silver are corroded. Their corrosion will testify against you and eat your flesh like fire. You have hoarded wealth in the last days. Look! The wages you failed to pay the workmen who mowed your fields are crying out against you. The cries of the harvesters have reached the ears of the Lord Almighty. You have lived on earth in luxury and self-indulgence. You have fattened yourselves in the day of slaughter. You have condemned and murdered innocent men, who were not opposing you.*
> ***James 5:1–6***

And, in what is perhaps the most disturbing of all the Bible's visions of future judgment, Revelation 18 describes the fate awaiting the city of Rome. Her obscene opulence while terrorizing the innocent (including, no doubt, Nero's massacre of Christians in the 60s AD) makes her doubly suited for divine punishment:

> *'Woe! Woe, O great city, where all who had ships on the sea became rich through her wealth! In one hour she has been brought to ruin! Rejoice over her, O heaven! Rejoice, saints and apostles and prophets! God has judged her for the way she treated you.'*
>
> *Then a mighty angel picked up a boulder the size of a large millstone and threw it into the sea, and said: 'With such violence the great city of Babylon will be thrown down, never to be found again. The music of harpists and musicians, flute players and trumpeters, will never be heard in you again. No workman of any trade will ever be found in you again. The sound of a millstone will never be heard in you again. The light of a lamp will never shine in you again. The voice of bridegroom and bride will never be heard in you again. Your merchants were the world's great men. By your magic spell all the nations were led astray. In her was found the blood of prophets and of the saints, and of all who have been killed on the earth.'*
> ***Revelation 18:19–24***

My point is simple: one of the most frequent and basic reasons given in the Bible for God's coming judgment is the reality of his compassion. God's fiery concern for the oppressed fuels his judgment upon oppressors.

God's judgment and the Messiah

Throughout the Bible, no individual is more closely associated with the execution of divine judgment than the Messiah. He is the one appointed by God to right the wrongs of the world. The Old Testament messianic prophecy of Isaiah 11 (quoted in the previous chapter) sums up the biblical perspective perfectly:

> *He will not judge by what he sees with his eyes, or decide by what he hears with his ears; but with righteousness he will judge the needy [i.e. on behalf of the needy], with justice he will give decisions for the poor of the earth. He will strike the earth with the rod of his mouth; with the breath of his lips he will slay the wicked.*
> ***Isaiah 11:3–4***

The Jewish Messiah, in other words, will be God's agent of judgment, defending the poor and overthrowing the unjust. He will embody God's fiery compassion for the oppressed and so execute God's judgment upon their oppressors.

Here we arrive at a frequently neglected, yet rather prominent, New Testament theme: the One entrusted with the judgment of the world is none other than Jesus, God's Messiah. There are so many passages we could reflect on. For instance, the apostle Peter declared in a sermon:

> *He [Jesus] commanded us to preach to the people and to testify that he is the one whom God appointed as judge of the living and the dead.*
> ***Acts 10:42***

The apostle Paul said pretty much the same thing:

This will take place on the day when God will judge men's secrets through Jesus Christ, as my gospel declares.
Romans 2:16

In an apocalyptic vision about the return of Jesus, John wrote in Revelation:

I saw heaven standing open and there before me was a white horse, whose rider is called Faithful and True. With justice he judges and makes war… The armies of heaven were following him, riding on white horses and dressed in fine linen, white and clean. Out of his mouth comes a sharp sword with which to strike down the nations… He treads the winepress of the fury of the wrath of God Almighty.
Revelation 19:11–15

It would be easy to think that these New Testament writers were simply getting carried away with their speculations about Jesus. In reality they were restating what they had heard from their Messiah's lips. By my count, there are close to a dozen occasions in the Gospels when Jesus affirms his role not only as the world's Saviour – which we will look at in Chapter 9 but also as its Judge.[60] Consider Jesus' words concerning certain Jewish towns that had rejected him and his message:

'Woe to you, Korazin! Woe to you, Bethsaida! For if the miracles that were performed in you had been performed in Tyre and Sidon [pagan cities], they would have repented long ago, sitting in sackcloth and ashes. But it will be more bearable for Tyre and Sidon at the judgment than for you. And you, Capernaum, will you be lifted up to the skies? No, you will go down to the depths.'[61]

One could almost say that Jesus was the original 'hell fire' preacher. The difference, of course, between him and the cliché some of us may have had the misfortune to endure is that Jesus delivered his message with a tear in his eye, not a smile on his face.[62]

One passage from Matthew's Gospel is especially interesting, for it reveals in the form of a parable both the *agent* of divine judgment and a central *criterion* of that judgment. Jesus' words are worth quoting in full:

> *When the Son of Man comes in his glory, and all the angels with him, he will sit on his throne in heavenly glory. All the nations will be gathered before him, and he will separate the people one from another as a shepherd separates the sheep from the goats. He will put the sheep on his right and the goats on his left. Then the King will say to those on his right, 'Come, you who are blessed by my Father; take your inheritance, the kingdom prepared for you since the creation of the world. For I was hungry and you gave me something to eat, I was thirsty and you gave me something to drink, I was a stranger and you invited me in, I needed clothes and you clothed me, I was sick and you looked after me, I was in prison and you came to visit me.'*
>
> *Then the righteous will answer him, 'Lord, when did we see you hungry and feed you, or thirsty and give you something to drink? When did we see you a stranger and invite you in, or needing clothes and clothe you? When did we see you sick or in prison and go to visit you?' The King will reply, 'I tell you the truth, whatever you did for one of the least of these brothers of mine, you did for me.'*
>
> *Then he will say to those on his left, 'Depart from me, you who are cursed, into the eternal fire prepared for the devil and his angels. For I was hungry and you gave me nothing to eat, I was thirsty and you gave me nothing to drink, I was a stranger and you did not invite me in, I needed clothes and you did not clothe me, I was sick and in prison and you did not look after me.' They also will answer, 'Lord, when did we see you hungry or thirsty or a stranger or needing clothes or sick or in prison, and did not help you?'. He will reply, 'I tell you the truth, whatever you did not do for one of the least of these, you did not do for me.' Then they will go away to eternal punishment, but the righteous to eternal life.*
> ***Matthew 25:31–46***

Perfectly in line with the Old Testament prophecies about the

Messiah, Jesus here declares that one day he will come in glory, sit on a heavenly throne (an image usually reserved for God alone, incidentally) and separate one person from another. He will speak the only words that will count on that day: 'Come, you who are blessed', or alternatively 'Depart from me, you who are cursed'. I do not know what your mental picture of Jesus Christ is, but it must be said, if only as a historical statement, that without some place for Christ's claimed role as the divine Judge, our image of him is, not to put it too strongly, imprecise.

Personally, the idea of Jesus as Judge both comforts and troubles me. On the one hand, I am reassured to know that someone as compassionate as Christ is entrusted with the judgment of our flawed humanity. On the other hand, I am acutely aware that this same Jesus thundered against religious hypocrisy and railed against the neglect of the needy. As a member of wealthy Western Christendom I must admit to feeling somewhat in the firing line of this aspect of Christ's teaching.

This brings us to the criterion of judgment, according to this passage. The thing separating the right from the left, the 'sheep' from the 'goats' or the 'blessed' from the 'cursed', is what they did or did not do, by action or neglect, for the plight of the destitute. Put positively, 'I was hungry and you gave me something to eat…' Put negatively, 'I was thirsty and you gave me nothing to drink.' How we treat the needy, in other words, is how we treat their Defender and Judge, the Messiah. A central criterion of divine judgment, according to Jesus, is how we care for the destitute and exploited.[63]

A couple of quick clarifications, and then I will bring this cheerless chapter to a close. Firstly, Jesus is not suggesting in this passage that salvation from judgment is secured by the performance of charity. Read in isolation I guess Matthew 25 could easily be taken that way. The problem is: there are too many other places in Jesus' teaching where he says that escaping divine wrath is a *gift* of divine mercy, not a reward for good behaviour.[64] The next chapter will underline this theme.

The quoted passage teaches what plenty of other New Testament texts teach: those who have received the gift of divine mercy commit themselves to lives of human mercy. The logic is summarized beautifully in Christ's words: 'Be merciful, just as your Father (God) is merciful'.[65] This connection between divine mercy and human mercy is so fundamental in Jesus' teaching that he can comfortably say that what separates the 'blessed' from the 'cursed' is the compassion they show to the destitute. The life of love, in other words, reveals those who have known the love of God. One is not saved by such a life but such a life marks those who are saved. That is the theory, anyway.

Secondly, the Bible's insistence that God will condemn those who have oppressed or neglected the needy does not mean that the needy are automatically exempt from judgment. While care for the oppressed is a central criterion of judgment, so is reverence for the Creator. Presumably, the poor and oppressed can fail this latter criterion and so find themselves under judgment for reasons other than that described in Matthew 25.[66]

Within the Bible's logic – and, of course, you and I are at liberty to dismiss this reasoning – just as revering the Creator while neglecting our fellow creatures leaves us culpable, so does caring for creatures while ignoring the Creator. What Christ required of humanity was that they 'love thy neighbour' *and* 'love thy Maker'.[67] To put it bluntly, but no less accurately from a historical perspective, Jesus would have condemned the philanthropic atheist with the same 'hell fire' gusto he directed at the religious hypocrite.[68]

Reflections

1. *The church and the needy*. Throughout the ages the belief that the Messiah will 'give decisions for the poor of the earth' (Isaiah 11:4) has inspired innumerable acts of charity within the church. In the early 30s AD the Jerusalem church set up a large daily food roster for destitute widows.[69] In the 40s and

50s AD the apostle Paul conducted what was perhaps the world's first truly international aid project, collecting money from the churches of Turkey, Greece and Macedonia for the famine-ravaged believers of Palestine.[70] By AD 250 the church in Rome was daily supporting 1500 destitute men, women and children.[71]

The influence of the ancient church's aid programs was so great that the fourth-century pagan Emperor Julian (AD 331–362) wrote to his pagan priests insisting that pagan temples introduce a welfare system modelled on the Christian one: hostels for strangers, orphanages and poverty relief projects. He wanted to beat the Christians, or 'Galileans' as he called them, at their own game. 'For it is disgraceful,' he complained to his high priest, 'that, when no Jew ever has to beg [because of Jewish welfare], and the impious Galilaeans support not only their own poor but ours as well, all men see that our people lack aid from us.'[72] Emperor Julian died the following year and his fear that the Christians might take over the empire through the stealth of compassion was soon realized.

Things in the church have not always proceeded in this way. I include the above material not only to highlight the historical influence of the theme of Christ as Judge but also to remind fellow believers of a part of their heritage that is sometimes forgotten. While it is still true that most non-government welfare in modern Australia is conducted by church agencies, often this work is so centralized that the average Christian can easily forget about his or her obligation toward the needy or, worse, decide to leave such work to 'head office'.

2. *Australians and the needy*. Contemporary Christians are not the only ones in the firing line, as it were, of Christ's pledge to bring justice for the needy. According to the Australian Bureau of Statistics' *Household Expenditure Survey* (2000), the average household in Australia spends a grand total of just $267 per annum on charitable giving, or $5.13 a week. That is just over half a per cent (0.58 per cent) of the average household income, or 58c per $100. The wealthier the household, the worse this figure gets.[73]

Compared to other expenditures the above figures are disturbing. Australian households annually spend more on their pets ($445.12), confectionary ($627.64), cigarettes ($503.36), beer and wine ($757.64), and restaurant and take-away meals ($1,733.16), than on charitable gifts ($267, as I said). Even in the face of the Asian tsunami of 2004–2005, the $150m raised by Australians in the fortnight following the disaster amounts to only $18.57 per household over the two week campaign. This figure belies talk at the time of 'extraordinary Australian generosity'.

Wider society, no less than the church community, would do well to reflect afresh, and seriously, on the words of the future Judge:

> *I was hungry and you gave me nothing to eat, I was thirsty and you gave me nothing to drink, I was a stranger and you did not invite me in, I needed clothes and you did not clothe me, I was sick and in prison and you did not look after me.*
> ***Matthew 25:42–43***

7 **Friend**
The scandal of his social life

I have described in detail in previous books how my introduction to the Christian faith came not through family tradition or church attendance but through the irresistible power of friendship and good food. My middle-aged Year 9 Scripture teacher had the courage one day to invite the entire class to her home for discussions about 'God'. The invitation would have gone unnoticed, except that she added: 'I'll be making hamburgers, milkshakes and scones.' The menu topped the chocolate bars my friends and I were pinching from the local supermarket most days after school, so one Friday afternoon several weeks later we found ourselves sitting on a comfy lounge in this woman's home with half-a-dozen other classmates feasting on her fantastic food and bracing ourselves for the god-part.

As I looked around the room I was amazed that this woman would open her home (and kitchen) to us. Some of the lads there that day were noted 'sinners' in our school: one was a drug user (and seller), one a class clown and bully, and another a petty thief with a string of break-and-enters to his credit. What was she thinking inviting us for a meal and discussion?

We returned the next Friday (with more hungry friends) and the next and the next. In fact, we turned up at this woman's house most Friday afternoons for the next year and a half. At no point was this teacher pushy or preachy. Her style was completely relaxed and incredibly generous. When her VCR went missing one day she made almost nothing of it, even though she suspected (reasonably enough) one of us had taken it.

For me, her open, flexible and generous attitude toward us 'sinners' was the doorway into understanding the significance of Christ. As we ate and drank and talked it was clear this was no mere missionary ploy on her part. She truly cared for us and treated us like friends or sons. Over the course of the next year she introduced me, as well as several others from the class, to the ultimate Friend of sinners, Jesus. Three of those lads are now clergymen.

My Scripture teacher embodied and illustrated for me one of the most striking dimensions of the ministry of the historical Jesus. Christ was famous in first-century Palestine for similar – though infinitely more significant – friendships with those classed as 'sinners'.

Sinners and ancient purity rules

'Sinners' were those in Jewish society who lived outside the laws of the Old Testament as interpreted by a first-century Jewish faction known as 'Pharisees' – probably from the Hebrew word *parush*, meaning 'separated', i.e. separated from all things impure. Sinners were not necessarily prostitutes, murderers and the like; they could just as easily be worldly businessmen who neglected synagogue attendance or conducted business with the occupying Romans (as the Jewish 'tax collectors' did). Sinners were the immoral and irreligious in a broadly moral and religious society.

In the Judaism of Jesus' day, contact with sinners was strictly regulated (especially by the Pharisees). To enter the home of a sinner or to have a sinner enter your home was to become tainted by their spiritual 'uncleanness'. In order to become 'clean' again, you would have to undergo a series of ritual washings. Even the house itself became 'unclean' through the presence of a sinner. In the collection of ancient rabbinic rulings known as the Mishnah – still a holy book in Orthodox Judaism, as mentioned earlier – we learn what happens when tax collectors, thieves or Gentiles (i.e. non-Jews) enter the home:

> *Concerning tax collectors who enter the house – the house is unclean. Concerning thieves who enter the house – only the place trodden by the feet of the thieves is unclean. And what do they render unclean? The foods, and the liquids, and the clay utensils which are open. But the couches and the seats and clay utensils which are sealed with a tight seal are clean. If there is a gentile with them, everything is unclean.*
> ***Mishnah Tohorot [Purities] 7:6***

Sharing *meals* with sinners (and Gentiles) was especially objectionable. In ancient societies, eating and drinking were powerful symbols of human fellowship. To share food and drink with people was to identify with them and, in a sense, to endorse them. Professor Graham Stanton of Cambridge University puts it well:

> *Sharing a meal with a friend today is often no more than a convenient way of consuming food. In the Graeco-Roman and Jewish world of the first century, however, eating food with another person was far more significant socially: it indicated that the invited person was being accepted into a relationship in which the bonds were as close as in family relations. One normally invited to meals only people whom one considered social and religious equals.*[74]

In a first-century Jewish setting, then, dining with sinners would be tantamount to endorsing their behaviour and so sharing their status.

Jesus, the 'Friend of sinners'

Jesus flouted these centuries-old customs. He regularly wined and dined with those considered to be moral and religious outcasts. He was so famous for this – or, perhaps, infamous – he came to be slandered in public. And, quite surprisingly from the historian's point of view, the insult is preserved in our Christian texts. In a passage from Matthew's and Luke's shared source (known as Q) Jesus' detractors are quoted as saying:

> *Here is a glutton and a drunkard, a friend of tax collectors and sinners.*
> ***Luke 7:34, Matthew 11:19***

That such a rumour could have arisen about Jesus seems strange to many today, but it did. And historians regard these scandalous dining habits as one of the most striking features of Christ's public ministry. Consider the following examples from the Gospels:

> *While Jesus was having dinner at Levi's house, many tax collectors and 'sinners' were eating with him and his disciples, for there were many who followed him. When the teachers of the law who were Pharisees saw him eating with the 'sinners' and tax collectors, they asked his disciples: 'Why does he eat with tax collectors and "sinners"?'*
> ***Mark 2:15–16***

> *Now the tax collectors and 'sinners' were all gathering around to hear him. But the Pharisees and the teachers of the law muttered, 'This man welcomes sinners and eats with them.'*
> ***Luke 15:1–2***

Or take an incident in Jericho, 30 km (18 miles) northeast of Jerusalem, where Jesus is said to have spotted a chief tax collector and invited himself to the man's home:

> *[Jesus] said to him, 'Zacchaeus, come down immediately. I must stay at your house today.' So he came down at once and welcomed him gladly. All the people saw this and began to mutter, 'He has gone to be the guest of a "sinner".'*
> ***Luke 19:5–7***

Of all the examples of this theme in Christ's life, perhaps none is more poignant than one found in Luke 7. In first-century

Palestine perhaps no one was considered more impure and deserving of divine judgment, in the opinion of first-century Jews, than a prostitute. And, yet, on at least one occasion, while dining at the home of a Pharisee, Jesus welcomed to the table a woman euphemistically introduced to us as having 'lived a sinful life in that town':

> *When a woman who had lived a sinful life in that town learned that Jesus was eating at the Pharisee's house, she brought an alabaster jar of perfume, and as she stood behind him at his feet weeping, she began to wet his feet with her tears. Then she wiped them with her hair, kissed them and poured perfume on them. When the Pharisee who had invited him saw this, he said to himself, 'If this man were a prophet, he would know who is touching him and what kind of woman she is – that she is a sinner.'*
> ***Luke 7:37–39***

The woman had heard Jesus was in town and in her desperation to meet him she 'gate-crashed' the home of a Pharisee – thus rendering the Pharisee's home 'unclean' according to rabbinic law. Much to the displeasure of the Pharisee and the other guests, Jesus let this woman touch him as she wept at his feet, hopeful of God's mercy. The touch itself would have rendered Jesus spiritually unclean in the eyes of many Jews. 'If this man were a prophet,' thought the Pharisee, 'he would know who is touching him and what kind of woman she is – that she is a sinner.'

Ironically, Jesus not only knew that the woman was a sinner, he knew what his host was thinking and responded by telling him a delightful, if somewhat unrealistic, hypothetical about a bank manager with two clients. One owed him the equivalent of $50,000, the other $5,000. Both debts were cancelled freely. 'Which of them will love the moneylender more?' asks Jesus. Let me continue the quotation from Luke 7:

> *Jesus answered him, 'Simon, I have something to tell you.'*
> *'Tell me, teacher,' he said. 'Two men owed money to a certain moneylender. One owed him five hundred denarii, and the other*

> *fifty. Neither of them had the money to pay him back, so he cancelled the debts of both. Now which of them will love him more?' Simon replied, 'I suppose the one who had the bigger debt cancelled.' 'You have judged correctly,' Jesus said. Then he turned toward the woman and said to Simon, 'Do you see this woman? I came into your house. You did not give me any water for my feet, but she wet my feet with her tears and wiped them with her hair. You did not give me a kiss, but this woman, from the time I entered, has not stopped kissing my feet. You did not put oil on my head, but she has poured perfume on my feet. Therefore, I tell you, her many sins have been forgiven – for she loved much. But he who has been forgiven little loves little.'*
> ***Luke 7:40–47***

The woman's extravagant act of devotion reveals her love for Jesus as the hoped-for source of divine forgiveness. Perhaps she had heard the rumours about this man who bypassed the temple priests and offered mercy to sinners directly and freely. Perhaps she had even heard Jesus preach, as she stood at the back of the crowd. Whatever drove her to seek out Jesus, she received the words she longed to hear, words I should think many would want to hear:

> *Then Jesus said to her, 'Your sins are forgiven.' The other guests began to say among themselves, 'Who is this who even forgives sins?' Jesus said to the woman, 'Your faith has saved you; go in peace.'*
> ***Luke 7:48–50***

In light of an incident like this, it is no wonder that Jesus' contemporaries – especially the religious leaders – slandered him as the 'Friend of sinners', a tag Jesus may well have taken as a compliment.

Judge and Friend: the paradox of Jesus' life

We are left with a paradox in the life of Jesus. The man who regularly proclaimed the coming judgment befriended those one might have thought were first in line for divine displeasure. The Judge of sinners was also the Friend of sinners.

According to the Gospels and the wider New Testament, this paradox was resolved in the death and resurrection of Jesus (studied in Chapters 9 and 10 below). Through these, Christ is said to have borne divine judgment for all who accept his hand of friendship. Jesus' openness toward sinners, then, was a deliberate sign of the welcoming grace of God. His preaching declared that grace, his suffering secured grace, and his scandalous social life embodied grace in a tangible way. Through his meals with the undeserving he sought to demonstrate the friendship with sinners he believed God so keenly desires.

Reflections

Let me unpack some of the ways Christian thought has, with varying degrees of success, appropriated this historical dimension of Christ's life.

1. *'Left' and 'right' in early Christianity*. Jesus' fraternizing with sinners heavily influenced the social conduct of the early church. Historians regularly point out that the first Christians completely overturned the social distinctions and attendant discrimination between Jew and Gentile, pure and impure, saint and sinner.

It was not that these disciples were all 'lefty relativists'. Far from it! Unlike modern society (and frequently modern Christendom), the ancient church was both right wing and left wing at the same time. The great divide in modern social discourse between left and right wing is, I think, one of the real intellectual blind spots of our culture, but that is perhaps for another book. The first Christians were utterly devoted to Jesus' ethical standards, which included some very clear guidelines on marriage, sex, honesty, etc., and at the same time utterly devoted to the social generosity Jesus had embodied. They ate with Gentiles and the immoral, they insisted that the rich among them should give honour (and assistance) to their poor brothers and sisters, they gladly accepted the shame of aligning themselves with people who were weak, sick and imprisoned, and their treatment of women – despite the current bad press on this issue – was positively enlightened.

The judgment of Rodney Stark, professor of sociology and comparative religion at University of Washington, has received wide approval among scholars:

> *Therefore, as I conclude this study, I find it necessary to confront what appears to me to be the ultimate factor in the rise of Christianity… The simple phrase 'For God so loved the world…' would have puzzled an educated pagan. And the notion that the gods care how we treat one another would have been dismissed as patently absurd… This was the moral climate in which Christianity taught that mercy is one of the primary virtues – that a merciful God requires humans to be merciful… This was revolutionary stuff. Indeed, it was the cultural basis for the revitalization of the Roman world groaning under a host of miseries… In my judgment, a major way in which Christianity served as a revitalization movement within the empire was in offering a coherent culture that was entirely stripped of ethnicity. All were welcome without need to dispense with ethnic ties… Christianity also prompted liberating social relations between the sexes and within the family…[and] greatly modulated class differences – more than rhetoric was involved when slave and noble greeted one another as brothers in Christ. Finally, what Christianity gave to its converts was nothing less than their humanity. In this sense virtue was its own reward.*[75]

None of this would have emerged within the ancient church if they had not been powerfully aware that their Teacher, Judge and Messiah was also a Friend to those normally excluded from society on moral and religious grounds.

2. *Being a friend of sinners*. When I was first learning about Christ, as a 15- to 16-year-old, I had no difficulty believing that God and Christians cared for me. This was so, even though I

knew I had not exactly lived the Christian life. The reason was that the main Christian in my life was the Scripture teacher I mentioned earlier, and she was the embodiment of a 'friend of sinners'.

On one occasion after a late night school party, one of my friends, David (not his real name), was heavily inebriated. Amid episodes of vomiting he begged us not to take him home, fearful of his father's reaction. One in our group came up with an idea, and I am embarrassed now as I recall it: 'Hey, doesn't the Scripture teacher live just down the road?'

Ten minutes later we were knocking on this woman's door interrupting her own dinner party. The fact that we all thought this was a perfectly reasonable idea at the time tells you what kind of person she seemed to us. The fact that she did not bat an eyelid tells you even more; and she was a strict teetotaller. She showed us in, let us throw David in the shower and provided him with some of her son's old clothes. Then she let us put him in one of the spare bedrooms for the night, as she went back to her guests. When we came to collect him the next morning about 10 a.m., there was the Scripture teacher cooking breakfast for David – not that he felt much like it!

When you have that kind of Christian in your life, believing that God, Christ and the church love sinners is easy. Of course, I later learnt how to doubt the divine love and look down on sinners myself, but that was only after mixing with some moralizing Christians for a while. In those early days I had no idea one could be bigoted and Christian at the same time.

My point is a simple one, and it has been borne out (and sometimes forgotten) time and again in the history of Christianity: those who know the Friend of sinners will be a friend to sinners.

8 Temple
The relocation of God's presence

There used to be a large sign on the northern side of the Australian town of Cooma which read: 'Cooma: Gateway to the Snowy Mountains'. I remember the excitement I felt as a child passing through Cooma on the way to our annual holiday in the New South Wales Snowy Mountains. My entire body would tingle with expectation as I wound down the window and felt the chilled mountain air streaming across my face. It is one of my most potent early childhood memories.

My sense of anticipation, however, was probably nothing compared with that of ancient Jews as they streamed toward Jerusalem for the annual Passover festival and arrived at the town of Bethphage – 'gateway to the holy city' – just 3 km (2 miles) from Jerusalem. Once pilgrims made their way up the road from Bethphage to the top of the Mount of Olives they would be greeted by a magnificent panoramic view of the holy city, just a kilometre or so away. At the front of their view was the huge Jerusalem temple, a site approximately the size of Stadium Australia.

The temple was the centre of Israel's national and religious life. This was where God chose to dwell, according to the Jewish Scriptures; it was where sacrifices for the forgiveness of sins could be made; it was where the country's leading teachers could be heard in the vast temple courts; it was where pilgrims gathered in their tens of thousands, especially at Passover time, to sing and pray to the one true God. For the devout Jew, arriving at the crest of the Mount of Olives and looking down at the temple of God must have stirred up extraordinary feelings of national pride and spiritual awe.

The donkey and the king

In the midst of this already heightened sense of occasion, toward the end of his public career as a teacher and healer, Jesus paused and told his disciples to do something that sounded suspiciously like the fulfilment of an Old Testament prophecy about the anointed descendant of King David. In the book of Zechariah (written around 500 years earlier) the prophet predicted that the long-awaited king would arrive in Jerusalem riding on a 'donkey':

> *Rejoice greatly, O Daughter of Zion! Shout, Daughter of Jerusalem! See, your king comes to you, righteous and having salvation, gentle and riding on a donkey, on a colt, the foal of a donkey... He will proclaim peace to the nations. His rule will extend from sea to sea and from the River to the ends of the earth.*
> ***Zechariah 9:9–10***

According to the Gospels, Jesus arranged to enter Jerusalem in April AD 30 mounted – you guessed it – on a donkey. To quote Matthew's version of the incident (which, like Luke's, is derived from the Gospel of Mark):

> *As they approached Jerusalem and came to Bethphage on the Mount of Olives, Jesus sent two disciples, saying to them, 'Go to the village ahead of you, and at once you will find a donkey tied there, with her colt by her. Untie them and bring them to me. If anyone says anything to you, tell him that the Lord needs them, and he will send them right away.'*
>
> *... The disciples went and did as Jesus had instructed them. They brought the donkey and the colt, placed their cloaks on them, and Jesus sat on them. A very large crowd spread their cloaks on the road, while others cut branches from the trees and spread them on the road. The crowds that went ahead of him and those*

> *that followed shouted, 'Hosanna to the Son of David!' 'Blessed is he who comes in the name of the Lord!' 'Hosanna in the highest!'*
> ***Matthew 21:1–9***[76]

The Zechariah prophecy just quoted was so well known that the disciples must have been bursting with excitement at the thought that finally, after being so coy about his status, Jesus was doing something overtly royal. The excitement spilled over into the crowd of pilgrims as they lay down cloaks and tree branches, the ancient equivalent of the red carpet, and began shouting in unison, 'Hosanna to the Son of David!'. The word Hosanna literally means 'Lord, save us now'. When combined with a reference to the son of King David, the expression carried powerful overtones about the arrival of a kingdom that would, according to the prophecy of Zechariah, 'extend from sea to sea and from the River to the ends of the earth'.

What the Gospels describe, then, is not a simple 'three cheers for Jesus'. This was a significant public parade acclaiming the man from Nazareth as the heir of the coming kingdom of God. For the first time, Jesus' authority as the messianic king was enthusiastically and publicly embraced. It must have been spine-tingling stuff. I am sure many readers remember the moment back in September 2000 when Australian athlete Cathy Freeman burst out in front in her 400 m Olympic final – the hopes of a nation on her shoulders. I suspect that moment pales in comparison to the excitement and expectation surrounding Jesus on this day in AD 30 as he rode into the holy city, right up to the great temple of God.

Jesus versus the temple

But, as so often in Christ's life, Jesus reinterpreted this grand expectation in a most unexpected way. The text from Matthew (like that of Luke and Mark) continues with Jesus' dramatic entry into the Jerusalem temple:

> *Jesus entered the temple area and drove out all who were buying and selling there. He overturned the tables of the moneychangers*

and the benches of those selling doves. 'It is written,' he said to them, '"My house will be called a house of prayer", but you are making it a "den of robbers".'
Matthew 21:12–13

According to the Gospels, Jesus did several unexpected, almost foolhardy, things in his encounter with the temple authorities, any one of which could have landed him in prison since – like a modern stadium – the Jerusalem temple had paid security guards.

In the first place, Jesus drove out those who were buying and selling. At Passover time families were required to make individual sacrifices of various animals. Rather than bring their own stock from home, pilgrims could purchase sacrificial animals on site. This began as a service but was very easily abused. When you are at a football stadium without any food or drink, you end up paying $5 for a bottle of water and $8 for a sandwich. When you were in Jerusalem at Passover time without a sacrificial animal, you were at the mercy of the priestly price. This so outraged Jesus that he drove them all out, making them pack up their stalls and leave the temple courts. How he pulled this off, we are not told. The main court of the temple where all these transactions took place was about 150 m long and 300 m wide (500 x 1,000 ft), and it would have been filled with pilgrims.

Secondly, Jesus overturned the tables of the moneychangers. These were temple accountants in charge of currency exchange. In this period all adult Jewish males had to pay an annual temple tax, handed over just before Passover. Temple officials, however, accepted only one currency, silver shekels of Tyre. So, before pilgrims could pay their dues they had to change their coins.[77] And, of course, there was a fee for the exchange. This too was open to abuse, and Jesus was appalled. Imagine the scene described above: tables overturned one by one, coins rolling across the temple court and crowds of the Jewish faithful standing around gob-smacked at the Teacher from Nazareth.

Jesus also overturned 'the benches of those selling doves'.

We might have thought the previous reference to 'those who were buying and selling' would have included those who sold doves. But these priestly salesmen are marked out for special attention in the Gospels. Why? Doves were sold to people who could not afford the usual sacrificial animals.[78] Dove sellers, then, were profiteering at the expense of the poor, and doing so in the name of religion. Given Christ's teaching about the obligation to care for the needy, it is no wonder his feelings reached boiling point. He overturned, we are told, not just the dove sellers' tables, but also their seats. In a very real sense, Jesus' actions against the temple were an expression of the messianic mission foretold in the Old Testament book of Isaiah (discussed in Chapter 5): 'with righteousness he will judge the needy, with justice he will give decisions for the poor of the earth'.[79]

Once Jesus had everyone's attention in this massive courtyard, he launched into a speech based on an Old Testament text (Isaiah 56:7): "My house will be called a house of prayer," Jesus said, "But you are making it a 'den of robbers'." These few words – which are just a summary of what he said – make it perfectly clear that Jesus believed the temple had become corrupt. There were more than 15,000 priests in Israel associated with the temple in this period and Jesus has just described them as a pack of thieves.

It is difficult to convey just how explosive all this must have been. Jesus has not simply interrupted a church service to offer a thought-for-the-day. He has first gone public with his status as the promised anointed king and then denounced the central feature of Israel's national and spiritual life – its glorious temple.

Jesus as the Temple

It is hardly surprising that Jesus would be dead by the end of the week. It is also not surprising that one of the central charges laid against him at his trial was his reported contempt for the temple. Matthew's Gospel records:

Finally two came forward and declared, 'This fellow said, "I am able to destroy the temple of God and rebuild it in three days".' Then the high priest stood up and said to Jesus, 'Are you not going to answer?'
Matthew 26:60–62

Jesus did not answer this charge, perhaps because he *did* actually say something like this – although he meant it in a symbolic way.[80] Historically revealing is the fact that in the Gospel of John's account of the clearing of the temple (written independently of the other three Gospels) we hear a statement from Jesus that comes very close to the one recalled at his trial:

Then the Jews demanded of him, 'What miraculous sign can you show us to prove your authority to do all this?' Jesus answered them, 'Destroy this temple, and I will raise it again in three days.' The Jews replied, 'It has taken forty-six years to build this temple, and you are going to raise it in three days?' But the temple he had spoken of was his body. After he was raised from the dead, his disciples recalled what he had said. Then they believed the Scripture and the words that Jesus had spoken.
John 2:18–22

At first sight, this is a bizarre statement: Jesus' body, crucified and raised, is the temple! However, this is not the first time Jesus has identified himself with the temple. The theme emerges a number of times in the Gospels. We get hints of it every time Jesus hands out divine forgiveness to people. In first-century Judaism, only the temple priests could pronounce forgiveness and even then, only after the appropriate sacrifice had been offered. This is why, after Jesus forgave the prostitute at the home of Simon the Pharisee, as discussed in the previous chapter, the guests murmured, 'Who is this who even forgives sins?' (Luke 7:49). Jesus handed out forgiveness whenever anyone humbly approached him. He acted as a kind of mobile temple.

An explicit comparison between Jesus and the temple is

found in Matthew 12 in a scene set about a year before Jesus took on the temple priests. The Pharisees had criticized Jesus' disciples for doing what looked like work on the Sabbath day. Jesus responded:

> *Haven't you read what David did when he and his companions were hungry? He entered the house of God, and he and his companions ate the consecrated bread – which was not lawful for them to do, but only for the priests. Or haven't you read in the Law that on the Sabbath the priests in the temple desecrate the day [i.e. do work on the Sabbath] and yet are innocent? I tell you that one greater than the temple is here.*
> ***Matthew 12:3–6***

The logic goes like this: priests are exempt from the Sabbath law when working within the precinct of the temple; how much more then are the disciples exempt when working in the proximity of the Messiah. Jesus, according to these words, is *more than the temple*, an extraordinary statement in its first-century context. Commenting on this theme, British New Testament historian N. T. Wright remarks: 'Jesus was taking the huge risk of acting as if he were the Shekinah [divine glory] in person, the presence of YHWH [God] tabernacling with his people.'[81]

Reflections

When Jesus rode into Jerusalem, entered the temple and declared its ministry bankrupt, he was not acting as a mere religious radical. According to the witness of the Gospel writers, he was acting as God's replacement temple. All that the temple had meant for Israel for almost 1000 years was now to be found in Israel's Messiah. The presence of God which human beings so longed for was to be found through a personal connection with Christ, not in a building in East Jerusalem. The hunger for divine teaching could be satisfied, not in the courts of a glorious sanctuary, but by feeding on the words of Jesus. True 'pilgrims' could henceforth declare their praises, not within the walls of one sacred building, but wherever people gathered in honour of the Messiah. And forgiveness of sins could be enjoyed through the one priestly sacrifice of Jesus, not through priest and sacrifice.

It is no wonder, then, that as Jesus breathed his last breath on the cross, just a week after his daring confrontation with the temple authorities, the inner sanctum of the temple itself was disturbed. As Matthew (following Mark) tells us:

> *And when Jesus had cried out again in a loud voice, he gave up his spirit. At that moment the curtain of the temple was torn in two from top to bottom.*
> ***Matthew 27:50–51***

The Jerusalem temple was eventually destroyed some 40 years after Jesus' death, when in August AD 70 Roman troops stormed Jerusalem to end a bitter five-year rebellion. All that remains of the temple is a 50-metre-long section of the western wall called the 'Wailing Wall'. Modern Jews congregate there to this day to cry out to God for the promised Messiah and for the restoration of God's holy sanctuary.

But from the point of view of the first followers of Jesus the temple was really overthrown and replaced in April AD 30. From the time of Christ's death and resurrection, said the early Christians, a new temple was established for all nations. All who want to locate the Creator's presence, learn his teaching and enjoy his forgiveness can do so simply by embracing the Messiah, the new temple.

9 Saviour
The meaning of his death

At fifteen years of age Samuel Peyton was sentenced to 'seven years' for the 'theft of a piece of cloth' – a frightening thought when I recall what I was getting up to at fifteen. Luckily, he was pardoned after just two years in prison. He would not be so lucky the second time around.

A couple of years later Peyton was caught in possession of a stolen watch, which he claimed he won in a card game. The explanation did not wash and he was sentenced to 'seven years transportation'. In May 1787 Samuel Peyton was bound for Sydney with 774 other convicts, chained in the hull of the *Alexander*.

On arriving at Sydney Cove eight months later Peyton was set to work as a stone mason supporting the flurry of early colonial building activity – the hospital, the prison and, of course, the Governor's House. Within five months the young Peyton was again in trouble. This time he was found in an officer's quarters trying to steal, so the report states, a 'shirt, stockings and a comb'. One gets the impression Samuel was more foolhardy than seriously evil.

Peyton was promptly tried and sentenced on Monday June 23rd 1788, and on Wednesday the 25th he was hanged on Sydney's public gallows where the exclusive Four Seasons Hotel now stands. He was just 21 years old.[82]

Samuel Peyton would be just another name in a convict log were it not for a letter he wrote to his mother, with the assistance of an unnamed friend, the night before his hanging. One of the First Fleet officers, Watkin Tench, was so taken with the letter that he copied it out in his own journal, which was later published.[83] Officer Tench was interested only in highlighting for his readership back in England 'that not the ignorant and untaught only have provoked the justice of their country to banish them to this remote region'. For me, though, Peyton's letter illustrates one of the most enduring legacies of the Gospels' portrait of Jesus. From the first century to the eighteenth century and beyond, people around the world have found in Christ a *Saviour*. Let me quote the letter:

> *My dear mother! with what agony of soul do I dedicate the few last moments of my life to bid you an eternal adieu: my doom being irrevocably fixed, and ere this hour tomorrow I shall have entered into an unknown and endless eternity. I will not distress your tender maternal feelings by any long comment on the cause of my present misfortune.*
>
> *Let it therefore suffice to say that impelled by that strong propensity to evil, which neither the virtuous precepts nor example of the best of parents could eradicate, I have at length fallen an unhappy, though just, victim to my own follies. Too late I regret my inattention to your admonitions, and feel myself sensibly affected by the remembrance of the many anxious moments you have passed on my account.*
>
> *For these and all my other transgressions, however great, I supplicate the Divine forgiveness; and encouraged by the promises of that Saviour who died for us all, I trust to receive that mercy in the world to come, which my offences have deprived me of in this.*
>
> *The affliction which this will cost you, I hope the Almighty will enable you to bear. Banish from your memory all my former indiscretions, and let the cheering hope of a happy meeting hereafter console you for my loss. Sincerely penitent for my sins; sensible of the justice of my conviction and sentence, and firmly relying on the merits of a Blessed Redeemer, I trust I shall yet experience that peace which this world cannot give.*
>
> *Commend my soul to Divine mercy. I bid you an eternal farewell.*
> *Your unhappy dying son,*
> *Samuel Peyton,*
> *Sydney Cove, Port Jackson,*
> *New South Wales, 24th June 1788*

This letter captures perfectly a theme of Christ's life that appears across the range of our earliest sources. To quote Peyton, Jesus is the 'Saviour who died for us all'.[84]

Saviour in life

In Chapter 5 we explored the meaning of Jesus' 'surname' – which, you will remember, was not a surname at all. 'Christ' (or in Hebrew: 'Messiah') is a title for the one 'anointed' to speak and act on God's behalf. But the Gospel writers gave another, equally important, title to Jesus. In fact, the two titles appear along aside each other in a passage usually associated with Christmas time:

> *I bring you good news of great joy that will be for all the people. Today in the town of David a Saviour has been born to you; he is Christ the Lord.*
> ***Luke 2:10–11***

If the title 'Christ' captured Jesus' status as the one endowed with divine authority, the title 'Saviour' captured Jesus' mission to rescue people from divine judgment.[85]

Even his given name conveyed this theme. 'Jesus', which is an Anglicized form of the Hebrew name Yeshua, translates as 'the Lord saves'. While in the modern world most of us are unaware of the meaning of our names, in antiquity, and especially in ancient Judaism, given names were transparent in meaning and highly significant. The Gospel of Matthew makes the point explicit:

> *She will give birth to a son, and you are to give him the name Jesus, because he will save his people from their sins.*
> ***Matthew 1:21***

My point is simple. According to the Gospels, by name as well as by title Jesus is the one who came to save men and women from divine judgment.

Here we arrive at one of the striking differences between

the first century and the twenty-first. Jesus lived in a culture so keenly aware of God's judgment that he had difficulty convincing people that sinners could be welcomed to the divine table. Ironically, it is probably under the influence of Jesus' teaching that many in contemporary society are so keen on the idea of God's love that now Christ would have difficulty convincing us that we were sinners in the first place.

But Jesus never taught that God will accept men and women because he is pleased with the way they are. Far from it. He insisted that humanity's incessant search for wealth at the expense of the poor is truly damnable.[86] He said that a person's love for the things of creation while ignoring the Creator himself is what makes him or her a 'sinner'.[87] And it is only against this backdrop that his title 'Saviour' can be understood. According to the Gospels, Jesus perceived his entire mission in terms of saving sinners from the coming judgment.

As we saw in Chapter 7, Jesus sought out those one might have thought were first in line for judgment, and he offered them mercy. To the prostitute who came to him in the Pharisee's house he declared 'Your faith has *saved* you; go in peace'.[88] To offer another potent example, as Jesus neared Jerusalem for his final week, he spotted a wealthy tax collector named Zacchaeus, someone who had been milking fellow Jews on behalf of the occupying Romans and creaming a fat profit off the top. According to the Gospel of Luke, Jesus invited himself to the man's home – much to the consternation of the religious – and made a statement that could easily stand as a banner over his entire mission:

> *Jesus said to him, 'Today salvation has come to this house, because this man, too, is a son of Abraham. For the Son of Man came to seek and to save what was lost.'*
> ***Luke 19:9–10***

The Saviour and his supper

The saviour theme reaches its climax in the final hours of Jesus' life, in his Last Supper and death on a cross. I stated in the previous chapter that Jesus arrived in Jerusalem during Passover week. At this time Jews from all over the Roman world made their pilgrimage to the holy city to take part in this most sacred day of the Jewish calendar. They were there to commemorate Israel's liberation from Egyptian slavery centuries before. A lamb would be sacrificed to recall the original Passover lamb whose blood was placed on the doorframes of Jewish homes. When God came in anger against the Egyptians that fateful night in the thirteenth century BC, he saw the blood of the lamb, says the Old Testament book of Exodus,[89] and preserved the Jewish families. His judgment fell upon Egypt but *passed over* the Jews. The Passover festival was a commemoration, in other words, of God saving his people. This is still its meaning among modern Jews.

Jesus managed to avoid arrest for most of Passover week. His days were spent speaking to large crowds of pilgrims in the temple courtyard, before slipping away at night to a friend's home a few kilometres east of Jerusalem. The final night was different. It was Passover Eve and Jesus wanted to celebrate this special occasion with his colleagues in the holy city itself.

When Jesus sat down to celebrate the Passover meal of April AD 30, things would have proceeded in much the same way as they had for the 1200 years before (and the 2000 years since): cooked lamb, traditional spices, wine, unleavened bread, prayers, songs, and so on. But Jesus added one highly unusual element that evening. He took the bread and wine in his hands and gave them an intriguing new meaning:

> *Jesus took bread, gave thanks and broke it, and gave it to his disciples, saying, 'Take and eat; this is my body.' Then he took the cup, gave thanks and offered it to them, saying, 'Drink from it, all of you. This is my blood of the covenant, which is poured out for many for the forgiveness of sins.'*
> ***Matthew 26:26–28***

Jesus took the traditional Passover themes of 'blood' and 'forgiveness' and related them to what is about to happen to him. Jesus' blood, just like that of the Passover lamb, would be poured out for the forgiveness of God's people. God's judgment would fall upon the 'lamb' (Jesus) so that it might pass over 'sinners'. This, according to Jesus, was his destiny. This was how the undeserving could be welcomed into his kingdom. This was how he would be the Saviour.

Within hours of this Last Supper, Jesus was arrested, put on trial and found guilty of 'blasphemy' and 'crimes against the temple'. However, at this time, Israel was an occupied territory. The Jewish leadership (mainly the priestly Sadducees) did not have the authority to administer the death penalty. That power lay with the Roman Procurator, Pontius Pilate, who saw in Jesus' claim to be Messiah a treasonous challenge to the authority of the Roman Emperor (Tiberius). In socio-political terms, then, it was the Romans who killed Jesus. But political explanations are only one way of looking at the event. The Gospels insist that the truest meaning of Jesus' death is found not in politics but in the Messiah's own explanation. Jesus died as a Saviour, the lamb for a worldwide 'Passover'.

The Saviour and his cross

Given the prominence of the 'saving' theme in the Gospels it is no wonder that, when Jesus is eventually tried and sentenced to death, the claim to be able to *save* people would be turned around as an insult. What kind of 'Saviour', reasoned his detractors, is unable to save himself? Luke's Gospel records how Jesus was mocked at the site of his crucifixion, a kilometre (0.6 miles) out of Jerusalem:

> *The people stood watching [the crucifixion], and the rulers even sneered at him. They said, 'He saved others; let him save himself if he is the Christ of God, the Chosen One.' The soldiers also came up and mocked him. They offered him wine vinegar and said, 'If you are the king of the Jews, save yourself.' There was a written notice above him, which read: THIS IS THE KING OF THE JEWS. One of the criminals who hung there hurled insults at him: 'Aren't you the Christ? Save yourself and us!'*
> ***Luke 23:35–39***

First the religious rulers, then the Roman soldiers, then one of the criminals crucified alongside Jesus: all draw attention to the irony of the situation. The one who claimed to save people from the coming judgment could not even save himself from the wrath of Rome.

As an historical aside, the ancient world interpreted Christ's crucifixion to be proof of the folly of Christianity. What kind of Saviour ends up naked on a Roman cross? As the apostle Paul lamented, 'the message of the cross is foolishness' in the eyes of the world.[90] This very perspective can be detected in the criticisms of Christ and Christianity found in the Roman writer Tacitus,[91] the Jewish Talmud[92] and the Greek satirist Lucian who dismisses the 'Saviour' of the Christians as 'that crucified sophist'.[93]

It must be remembered that the ancients regarded crucifixion as the most shameful of deaths. Of the three main methods of execution – decapitation, burning and crucifixion – crucifixion was considered the most severe, and Roman citizens were officially exempt from ever undergoing it. The Roman writer and statesman, Cicero (106–43 BC), described crucifixion as the *summum supplicium*, the 'ultimate punishment'.[94] A century later the Roman philosopher Seneca (4 BC–AD 65) described the fate of crucifixion in the following way:

> *Can anyone be found who would prefer wasting away in pain dying limb by limb, or letting out his life drop by drop, rather than expiring once for all? Can any man be found willing to be fastened to the accursed tree, long sickly, already deformed, swelling with ugly weals on shoulders and chest, and drawing the breath of life amid long-drawn-out agony? He would have many excuses for dying even before mounting the cross.*
> **Seneca, *To Lucilius, Epistle 101***

One can see in such texts the very real dilemma faced by the first Christians as they tried to convince the Roman world that a crucified man was the Lord and Saviour of the world.[95] The fact that they pulled it off is an even greater historical puzzle, but one that lies beyond the scope of this book.

What many saw as a shameful failure, paradoxically, was viewed as a beautiful victory by those who really knew what Jesus taught. It was precisely in *not* saving himself from the cross that Jesus became the Saviour of the world. In a twist of outcomes that can be seen only through the lens of Jesus' teaching, sinners could be saved from God's judgment only because the Saviour bore that judgment himself.

According to Luke's Gospel, at least one person who was there when Christ was crucified spotted this paradox. Hearing the mockery of the leaders, soldiers and the criminal, a second criminal, himself facing the *summum supplicium*, rebuked the first and turned to Jesus as Saviour:

> *But the other criminal rebuked him [i.e. the first criminal]. 'Don't you fear God,' he said, 'since you are under the same sentence? We are punished justly, for we are getting what our deeds deserve. But this man has done nothing wrong.' Then he said, 'Jesus, remember me when you come into your kingdom.' Jesus answered him, 'I tell you the truth, today you will be with me in paradise.'*
>
> *It was now about the sixth hour, and darkness came over the whole land until the ninth hour, for the sun stopped shining. And the curtain of the temple was torn in two. Jesus called out with a loud voice, 'Father, into your hands I commit my spirit.' When he had said this, he breathed his last.*
>
> ***Luke 23:40–46***

For as long as I have known the Gospels I have loved these words. There is no religion here; no complex theology – just a simple admission of unworthiness and a daring, though insightful, request for mercy. One struggles to think how anyone could have believed in that moment that Jesus possessed a 'kingdom' – he certainly would not have looked very royal at that time. However he worked it out, this criminal saw what others missed: not saving himself was exactly how Jesus would save others. And in that perceptive moment he received one of the clearest promises of 'salvation' in the Bible: 'I tell you the truth, today you will be with me in paradise.'

Reflections

Whenever believers have doubted that Christ's death on the cross was enough to win God's forgiveness, cancel their judgment and guarantee them a place in God's kingdom, Jesus' promise to a dying sinner has offered ample proof that he is the Saviour of all who humbly trust him.

This is what the young convict Samuel Peyton meant when he wrote to his mother almost 1800 years later:

> *Encouraged by the promises of that Saviour who died for us all, I trust to receive that mercy in the world to come, which my offences have deprived me of in this.*

Peyton's hanging is mentioned in several journals of the time. It was a cold, wet and squally June day. At 11:30 am the 21-year-old mounted the gallows and made what one witness describes as 'an eloquent and well-directed speech' in which he admitted his guilt and asked forgiveness from those he had wronged. He 'died penitent', says another witness. Christians would say he died in the embrace of the Saviour.

Christianity has always declared that Jesus died for petty thieves like Samuel Peyton, for Jewish rebels like the man crucified with Jesus, for neglectful materialists, for thankless atheists, for the morally self-righteous and even for the smugly religious. For any who sincerely turn back to God, so says the New Testament and the Christian church ever since, Christ is the 'Saviour who died for us all'.

10 Adam
The promise of his resurrection

Concerning the resurrection of Jesus on Easter Sunday, I was for decades a Sadducee [a Jewish sect which denies the afterlife]. I am no longer a Sadducee since the following deliberation has caused me to think this through anew... [W]hen these peasants, shepherds, and fishermen, who betrayed and denied their master and then failed him miserably, suddenly could be changed overnight into a confident mission society, convinced of salvation and able to work with much more success after Easter than before Easter, then no vision or hallucination is sufficient to explain such a revolutionary transformation... If the defeated and depressed group of disciples overnight could change into a victorious movement of faith, based only on autosuggestion or self-deception – without a fundamental faith experience – then this would be a much greater miracle than the resurrection itself. In a purely logical analysis, the resurrection of Jesus is 'the lesser of two evils' for all those who seek a rational explanation of the worldwide consequences of that Easter faith.[96]

This quotation comes not from a clergyman or a Christian scholar but from the late Professor Pinchas Lapide, a German New Testament historian and Orthodox Jew. That a devout Jew – contrary to his religious tradition – could conclude on historical grounds that Jesus rose again from the dead does not, of course, prove anything. It does, however, illustrate something that may surprise some readers. The resurrection of Jesus remains a topic of serious enquiry among specialists in the field.[97]

It is not my intention to prove that Jesus rose from the dead: I have said all along, this is not that kind of book. I do, however, want to demonstrate that the resurrection is both an unavoidable theme of the earliest sources *and* an indispensable aspect of the Christian worldview ever since. It is no exaggeration to say that without the resurrection there is no Christianity. As the apostle Paul remarked in a moment of surprising candour: 'if Christ has not been raised, our preaching is useless and so is your faith... we are to be pitied more than all men' (1 Corinthians 15:14, 19).

Raised expectations?

Prior to April AD 30 no one in the ancient world – Jewish or pagan – would have expected a crucified Teacher such as Jesus to rise again from the dead. It was simply not part of anyone's job description for greatness. This point is frequently overlooked in popular discussions of the topic but it gives historians pause.

It is true that some pagans celebrated rituals of dying-and-rising gods (typically as a symbol of the cycles of fertility and harvest) but no one in these cultures ever thought this was an event that took place in time and space or that human beings could experience this dying and rising.[98] Indeed, scholars have often pointed out that such an idea would have been preposterous in Greco-Roman thought since, for various complicated philosophical reasons, pagans excluded the possibility of a post-mortem existence that was physical.[99]

Unlike their pagan neighbours, many Jews in the period did believe in a bodily life-after-death. However, they did so in a manner that virtually ruled out any expectation that someone would rise from the dead in AD 30. Traditional Jewish teaching, both before and after Jesus,[100] stated that at the *end of history* the faithful dead would rise to eternal life in a divinely restored creation. This was a central part of the Jewish hope for God's future kingdom (which, you may remember from Chapter 3, Jesus fully endorsed). Belief in a general resurrection in the 'kingdom come' is everywhere in Jewish writings of the time: in the Dead Sea Scrolls, Josephus, the Pseudepigrapha, the Apocrypha, and elsewhere. The belief was founded on an important passage in the Old Testament book of Daniel:

> *But at that time your people – everyone whose name is found written in the book – will be delivered. Multitudes who sleep in the dust of the earth will awake: some to everlasting life, others to shame and everlasting contempt. Those who are wise will shine like the brightness of the heavens, and those who lead many to righteousness, like the stars for ever and ever. But you, Daniel, close up and seal the words of the scroll until the time of the end.*
> ***Daniel 12:1–3***

This theme of 'resurrection of the dead' (in the future kingdom) remains a part of Orthodox Judaism to this day. The important point to observe, however, is that resurrection in Judaism, ancient and modern, is something that will happen at the conclusion of human history, not in the middle of it. It is an event at 'the time of the end' as Daniel put it. Any claim that an individual had experienced bodily resurrection *before* the arrival of God's kingdom was not only unexpected; it was deeply counter-intuitive within a Jewish perspective.

The early Christian claim that their Saviour had experienced the future resurrection *in advance*, as it were, is completely without precedent in both Jewish and Greco-Roman cultures of antiquity. Certainly, something other than existing expectations gave rise to the claim.

Adding to the scholarly conundrum over what might have prompted the first Christians to make claims about a resurrection is what we know of Jewish martyrdom. Ever since the Jewish revolts against Greek domination in the 160s BC (called the Maccabean wars), a strong tradition in Judaism paid special honour to faithful Jews slain by pagan overlords. Such people were praised in popular legends and their tombs became sites of religious veneration. By the time the Romans ruled Palestine (from 63 BC) this tradition was firmly established in Jewish consciousness. Scholars frequently comment upon the significance of this observation. If the New Testament had left Jesus in a martyr's tomb, this would have been a perfectly respectable way to conclude a story about a great Jewish teacher. There was no need, in other words, to invent a resurrection story in order to secure Jesus' fame. The fact that the pagan Romans executed him would have virtually guaranteed him a place in the roll call of faithful Jewish martyrs.[101] Yet, from the earliest period, the disciples made no attempt to cast Jesus as a heroic martyr. And, as far as we can tell, his tomb was never a site of religious devotion.[102] Instead, contrary to all expectations, the first Christians insisted that the tomb in which Jesus was laid on Friday afternoon was empty come Sunday morning.

Explanations abound, of course. Perhaps Jesus' followers stole the body and kept quiet about it all the way to their imprisonment and death (frequently by martyrdom). This was the Jewish leadership's counter-claim about the resurrection,[103] which in part is why modern scholars are confident Jesus' tomb really was empty shortly after his crucifixion: otherwise, this Jewish retort would not have arisen. Another popular explanation is that Jesus did not really die on the cross; he recovered from his injuries, walked out of the tomb and convinced his disciples that God had granted him the glorious resurrection life awaiting all the faithful.[104] Such explanations are entirely rational on the assumption, mentioned in Chapter 3, that the observable laws of nature are the only forces active in the universe. But, of course, the early Christians did not share this assumption. The empty tomb, combined with numerous reports that Jesus had appeared alive to his followers, convinced them that God had indeed raised his Messiah from the dead: the end-time resurrection had broken into history in the events surrounding Jesus. Their claim launched a movement that would utterly transform the world.

The earliest resurrection report

As I said earlier, reports about the resurrection appear throughout the range of our New Testament sources. At the end of the chapter I will offer some readings from the Gospels' resurrection accounts. For now, I want to focus on what historians regard as the most significant text about the resurrection.

In his letter to the newly founded church at Corinth, the apostle Paul reminds his converts of the core message (called the 'gospel') he preached to them five years earlier. He does not expound the message in full; instead, he offers a fixed summary designed to recall the major elements of the preaching of the original apostles.

The verses quoted below contain what scholars universally regard as the earliest 'creed' in Christianity. A creed is a pithy statement of what someone believes (*credo* is Latin for 'I believe'). Some of you may have heard of the Apostles' Creed, which is said to this day in Roman Catholic and Protestant churches all over the world. The Apostles' Creed began to be formulated in the third century AD but the creed found in Paul's letter to the Corinthians was composed and handed on to the apostle as early as AD 34, just a few years after Jesus' crucifixion.[105] Paul (and others) used this creed as a bullet-point summary of their gospel. It was handed on to Christian communities as an official reminder of the founding message. Paul indeed describes it as something 'of first importance':

> *Now, brothers, I want to remind you of the gospel I preached to you, which you received and on which you have taken your stand. By this gospel you are saved, if you hold firmly to the word I preached to you. Otherwise, you have believed in vain. For what I received I passed on to you as of first importance:*
>
> *that Christ died for our sins according to the Scriptures,*
> *that he was buried,*
> *that he was raised on the third day according to the Scriptures,*
> *and that he appeared to Peter, and then to the Twelve.*

After that, he appeared to more than five hundred of the brothers at the same time, most of whom are still living, though some have fallen asleep. Then he appeared to James, then to all the apostles, and last of all he appeared to me also, as to one abnormally born.
1 Corinthians 15:1–8

The above statement is significant for historians not simply because part of it constitutes an eyewitness claim ('he appeared also to me') but, more importantly, because of the date of the report – early to mid 30s AD in the opinion of most mainstream scholars. This establishes beyond doubt that the claim about the resurrection belonged to the earliest stage of Christianity. It is not an extraneous belief inserted into the Gospels later; it was the bedrock of the Jesus-movement post AD 30. Whatever our personal feelings about 'resurrections', there is no avoiding the historical conclusion that this claim has always been at the core of what we call Christianity. James Dunn, Emeritus Professor of New Testament at University of Durham, makes the point well:

That belief seems to have been not only fundamental for Christianity as far back as we can trace, but also presuppositional and foundational. Any claims to disentangle a Jesus movement or form of Christianity which did not celebrate Jesus' resurrection inevitably have to assume what they are trying to prove, since all the data available (including Q) were retained by churches which did celebrate his resurrection. As a historical statement we can say quite firmly: no Christianity without the resurrection of Jesus.[106]

Resurrection appearances and an empty tomb

According to the above passage, the resurrected Jesus appeared to at least six different individuals or groups of disciples:

1. To *Cephas*, the Aramaic equivalent of the Greek name Peter;
2. To the *twelve* apostles together;
3. To *500 of the brothers* at once;

4. To *James*, Jesus' brother;
5. To *all of the apostles*, that is, to missionaries beyond the group of the twelve;
6. To the apostle *Paul*, who had been a persecutor of the Christians up to that moment.

Interestingly, there was another set of witnesses not mentioned in the above report. According to all four Gospels, the first people to witness the empty tomb and the risen Jesus were not the (male) apostles but a small group of women, including Mary (Jesus' mother), Salome, Joanna and (another) Mary.[107] For historians, this is an intriguing detail since the testimony of women was seriously questioned in both Jewish and Greco-Roman cultures of the time. Josephus, writing in the first century, reflects the views of many in his day: 'From women let no evidence be accepted, because of the levity and temerity of their sex.'[108] Commenting on this detail James Dunn wrote recently:

> *Yet, as is well known, in Middle Eastern society of the time women were not regarded as reliable witnesses: a woman's testimony in court was heavily discounted. And any report that Mary had formerly been demon-possessed (Luke 8:2) would hardly add credibility to any story attributed to her in particular. Why then attribute such testimony to women – unless that was what was remembered as being the case? In contrast, can it be seriously argued that such a story would be contrived in the cities and/or village communities of first-century Palestine, a story which would have to stand up before public incredulity and prejudice? This consideration alone may be sufficient to explain why the tradition cited by Paul [i.e. in 1 Corinthians 15 quoted above] does not include the testimony of women in its list of witnesses.*[109]

Put simply, if one were making up a story about a resurrection and wanting fellow first-century Jews to believe it, one would not include women as the initial witnesses. The point is worth reflecting on. It was once argued in scholarship that the Gospel accounts of the discovery of the empty tomb were late inventions crafted to lend narrative weight to the apostles' claims that they had seen Jesus alive. The view has lost adherents in the last decade (even among sceptical scholars) since several features of the accounts (the involvement of the women being just one example) would actually have weakened the strength of the claim in a first century context.[110] On the whole, the Gospels read like honest attempts to relate what the followers of Jesus had affirmed from the very beginning. Whatever our personal feelings about the resurrection, it is difficult to avoid the historical conclusion that the empty tomb and the testimony of the women (along with that of the apostles) were core parts of Christianity from its inception.

What historians can and cannot conclude

Let me repeat something I said in connection with Jesus' healings in Chapter 3. By its nature, historical enquiry cannot determine whether a particular miraculous event took place. The best we can do is determine: (a) how early the reports about a supposed miraculous event are, i.e. whether the time gap between the event and the first report was sufficient for it to be explained as a mere 'legend'; (b) how widespread the reports are, i.e. how many independent sources make the same claim; and (c) whether such claims can be explained by cultural expectation or precedent. In the case of the healings, you may remember, I stated that historians cannot affirm (or deny) Jesus *actually* healed anyone – that would be to go beyond historical method to philosophical interpretation. What historians can (and do) affirm is that the reports of Jesus' healings are early, widespread and without cultural precedent. This invites the mainstream scholarly conclusion that those around him interpreted Christ's activities as supernatural.

Roughly the same historical conclusion can be reached about the resurrection. Historians cannot demonstrate that Jesus actually rose from the dead. All they can do is demonstrate that the reports about the resurrection are very early, widespread and completely without cultural expectation or precedent. Two conclusions are thus drawn by a majority of mainstream scholars:

1. Jesus' tomb was very likely empty shortly after his crucifixion, and;
2. From the very beginning, significant numbers of men and women claimed to have seen Christ alive from the dead.[111]

How people account for these two historical data will depend largely on what one feels is possible in the world. As discussed in Chapter 3, if I assume that the observable laws of nature are the only forces active in the universe, then, I may rationally affirm that no evidence can be good enough to overturn the conclusion that dead people stay dead. I will therefore opt for whatever I believe to be the most plausible naturalistic interpretation.[112] If, on the other hand, I assume that the observable laws of nature are *not* the only forces active in the universe – that there is behind these laws a Law-giver – then, I may rationally interpret the historical data as evidence for an actual resurrection, at least in the case of Jesus (since no comparable data exist for any other character in history).

Basically, then, whether one concludes that Jesus rose again depends in the end not on historical questions but (principally) on one's beliefs about God. Eminent New Testament scholar Professor Graham Stanton of Cambridge University puts the point bluntly. After traversing much of the same ground covered above, he concludes:

> *The early Christian claim was that God raised the crucified, dead, and buried Jesus 'on the third day' to a new form of existence, the precise nature of which Paul and the four evangelists describe in rather different ways. That claim can be neither confirmed nor denied with the use of historical lines of inquiry. Whether it may be accepted as plausible depends both on careful assessment of the resurrection traditions and on convictions about God.*[113]

'Adam': the meaning of the resurrection

Readers may be wondering why I titled this chapter 'Adam'; so far, I have said nothing about the ancient story told in the opening chapters of the Bible. The first Christians interpreted the resurrection in a variety of ways, as they began to make sense of something completely without precedent and entirely unexpected.[114] One of the earliest and most significant interpretations is found in Paul's letter to the Corinthians, in a passage following on from the gospel 'creed' discussed earlier. Here, the apostle says the resurrection establishes Jesus as the founding member of a revived humanity in God's long-awaited kingdom. Jesus, in other words, is the new 'Adam':

> *But Christ has indeed been raised from the dead, the firstfruits of those who have fallen asleep. For since death came through a man, the resurrection of the dead comes also through a man. For as in Adam all die, so in Christ all will be made alive. But each in his own turn: Christ, the firstfruits; then, when he comes, those who belong to him. Then the end will come, when he hands over the kingdom to God the Father after he has destroyed all dominion, authority and power.*
> ***1 Corinthians 15:20–24***

There is so much we could explore in this passage (entire PhDs have been written on this section of Paul's letter). For 'spectators', though, a few things are worth noting. Firstly, Paul describes the risen Jesus as the 'firstfruits', an agricultural term for the initial produce of a coming harvest. What does this mean? As a Jew, Paul had been brought up believing that resurrection was a *future* experience for the *whole* of humanity (the idea of departed souls entering an eternal, ethereal existence was pagan not Jewish). Jews hoped for a resurrected humanity in a renewed creation.[115] In the passage just quoted Paul is trying to reconcile this Jewish theology with his encounter with the risen Christ. Jesus, says Paul, is the firstfruits of God's great future harvest when he revives the dead and renews the world. What God had promised to do at the end of history, he has demonstrated within history in raising Jesus from the dead.

As the firstfruits Jesus is also a kind of 'Adam' figure, Paul says. Again, the apostle is operating here in a thoroughly Jewish (Old Testament) frame of mind. According to the opening chapters of the Scriptures, the entire history of humanity could be observed in the actions of the first human being.[116] Adam was fashioned by the loving hands of the Creator only to turn his back on the Almighty, preferring personal autonomy instead of a relationship with God. The story of Adam eating from the 'tree of the knowledge of good and evil' has nothing to do with gluttony or sensuality; it is all about Man wanting to determine for himself, without God's involvement, what the parameters of 'good and evil' should be. Whatever one's view of the origin of our species, the Genesis narrative is deeply true and deliberately universal. This point is underlined by the fact that 'Adam' in Hebrew means simply *Man* or *Mankind*.

Paul's point in referring to this Old Testament narrative is clear. What Adam was to world history, Jesus is to God's future kingdom: the progenitor and paradigm of a new humanity. Jesus is the original of the species, as it were, and he determines our destiny.

Also important is Paul's mention of God's 'kingdom'. Here, Paul reflects both Jewish beliefs and Jesus' teaching. In Chapter 3 we saw that Jesus proclaimed a *future* kingdom when all creation would be brought into conformity to the wise and loving purposes of the Creator. In this sense, he was perfectly in line with classical Judaism, ancient and modern. On one or two occasions, however, as we saw, Jesus said that the future kingdom was somehow present in his ministry of healing and exorcism: 'the kingdom of God has come upon you', he said (Matthew 12:28). In other words, what was usually described in the Bible as an ultimate future reality could be glimpsed in Jesus' startling deeds. The apostle Paul says Christ's *resurrection* functions in a similar way. It is a glimpse of God's future kingdom. The Old Testament pledge to raise the dead and revive creation at the end of history finds a divine guarantee – a down payment, you might say – *within history* in the resurrection of the Messiah.

Far more than vindication of a righteous man or a proof of the Messiah, the resurrection of Jesus is the Creator's first act of bringing all creation into conformity to his purposes. It anticipates the day when, as Paul says above, Christ will have 'destroyed all dominion, authority and power'. Jesus is 'Adam' in God's new kingdom.

Reflections

From the very beginning, the resurrection of Christ decisively shaped the Christian view of the 'afterlife'. This is illustrated well by the Apostles' Creed, which has been a standard statement of belief since its origins in the third century. To this day all Roman Catholics and Protestants affirm the Apostles' Creed, making it an extraordinarily ecumenical statement. In any case, there are two references in this creed to the 'afterlife'. One relates to Jesus, the other to Christians in general. Both concern the absolutely essential idea of bodily resurrection. To quote the creed in full (originally in Latin and Greek):

I believe in God, the Father almighty,
creator of heaven and earth.
I believe in Jesus Christ, God's only Son, our Lord,
who was conceived by the Holy Spirit,
born of the Virgin Mary,
suffered under Pontius Pilate,
was crucified, died, and was buried;
he descended to the dead.
On the third day he rose again;
he ascended into heaven,
he is seated at the right hand of the Father,
and he will come again to judge the living and the dead.
I believe in the Holy Spirit,
the holy catholic church,
the communion of saints,
the forgiveness of sins,
the resurrection of the body,
and the life everlasting. Amen.

Sometimes people assume, even those who have attended church for a long time, that the reference at the end of the creed to 'the resurrection of the body and the life everlasting' simply reiterates what is said earlier about the resurrection of Jesus. A moment's thought, however, makes clear that the final lines of this ancient summary of Christian belief refer to the faithful, not Jesus. Following the New Testament's teaching, the Apostles' Creed states that just as 'on the third day he (Jesus) rose again' so at the end of history men and women will experience 'the resurrection of the body'. And it is in that bodily mode that the faithful will enjoy 'the life everlasting'. Historically, the Christian view of the afterlife has always involved resurrected bodies in a revived creation. That is what the kingdom of God is.

Here we arrive at one of the distinctive elements of the biblical understanding of the future. Eastern traditions such as Hinduism and Buddhism respond to the frailties and disappointments of the natural order by holding out the eternal hope of *nirvana* (literally, 'blown-out'), a state of absolute non-physicality.[117] For these philosophies, physical reality is not reality at all; rather it is an entrapment from which we will finally free ourselves. Biblical hope is radically different. When the Bible describes the future kingdom of God – what we commonly call 'heaven' – it speaks not of the removal of physical existence but of its re-creation. The natural world will be liberated and the human body redeemed. Consider these words from the apostle Paul:

> *The creation itself will be liberated from its bondage to decay and brought into the glorious freedom of the children of God. We know that the whole creation has been groaning as in the pains of childbirth right up to the present time. Not only so, but we ourselves, who have the firstfruits of the Spirit, groan inwardly as we wait eagerly for our adoption as sons, the redemption of our bodies.*
> ***Romans 8:21–23***

For many of us I suspect our picture of the 'kingdom come' derives from an unlikely combination of ancient Greek philosophy and modern Hollywood movies. The ancient

Greek philosopher Plato taught that the physical world is a kind of grubby reflection of the ultimate non-physical reality toward which everything is destined. Somehow, Hollywood got hold of this idea and now almost always portrays the afterlife as a fourth-dimensional existence with clouds, halos, bright lights and the ever-present harp music. 'Bodies' are conspicuous by their absence.

In the years after I first learnt about Christ, it always troubled me that I was now meant to enjoy the thought of escaping the physical world and entering a spiritual one called heaven. I loved the taste, smell, sight, sound and touch of this world, and now I was meant to look forward to losing those five senses and having them replaced by a spiritual sixth sense. I was not terribly excited about it.

Fortunately, I soon learnt that this was not what Christianity affirms about the afterlife at all. The biblical 'kingdom come' is not an ethereal place of clouds and ghosts, but a tangible place of real existence. Far from the Hollywood notion of a disembodied, nirvana-like bliss, the Old and New Testaments promise a 'new creation' and a 'resurrection of the body'.[118]

The vision of the 'kingdom come' that historic Christianity has proclaimed is not a ghostly existence, which denies the reality of creation, but a bodily existence in which the frailties and disappointments of the natural order are resolved through an extraordinary act of divine re-creation. If readers are wondering what all this has to do with the topic of Christ's resurrection, the answer is simple: Christ's rising to life is central to biblical faith not merely because it marks out his life as a unique moment in history, but because in it God shows he is willing and able to breathe new life where there is currently death and disorder.

According to almost two millennia of Christian reflection on the bizarre events of April AD 30, the resurrection of Jesus is God's tangible pledge within history that he intends to do the same for the whole creation at the end of history. It is on this basis that Christianity from the earliest days proclaimed Jesus as 'Adam' and invited the world to become part of the new humanity he has promised.

A selection of readings on the resurrection of Christ

Luke 24:1–47

On the first day of the week, very early in the morning, the women took the spices they had prepared and went to the tomb. They found the stone rolled away from the tomb, but when they entered, they did not find the body of the Lord Jesus. While they were wondering about this, suddenly two men in clothes that gleamed like lightning stood beside them. In their fright the women bowed down with their faces to the ground, but the men said to them, 'Why do you look for the living among the dead? He is not here; he has risen! Remember how he told you, while he was still with you in Galilee: "The Son of Man must be delivered into the hands of sinful men, be crucified and on the third day be raised again."' Then they remembered his words. When they came back from the tomb, they told all these things to the Eleven and to all the others. It was Mary Magdalene, Joanna, Mary the mother of James, and the others with them who told this to the apostles. But they did not believe the women, because their words seemed to them like nonsense. Peter, however, got up and ran to the tomb. Bending over, he saw the strips of linen lying by themselves, and he went away, wondering to himself what had happened.

Now that same day two of them were going to a village called Emmaus, about seven miles from Jerusalem. They were talking with each other about everything that had happened. As they talked and discussed these things with each other, Jesus himself came up and walked along with them; but they were kept from recognizing him. He asked them, 'What are you discussing together as you walk along?' They stood still, their faces downcast. One of them, named Cleopas, asked him, 'Are you only a visitor to Jerusalem and do not know the things that have happened there in these days?' 'What things?' he asked. 'About Jesus of Nazareth,' they replied. 'He was a prophet, powerful in word and deed before God and all the people. The chief priests and our rulers handed him over to be sentenced to death, and they crucified him; but we had hoped that he was the one who was going to redeem Israel. And what is more, it is the third day since all this took place. In addition, some of our women amazed us. They went to the tomb early this morning but didn't find his body. They came and told us that they had seen a vision of angels, who said he was alive. Then some of our companions went to the tomb and found it just as the women had said, but him they did not see.'

He said to them, 'How foolish you are, and how slow of heart to believe all that the prophets have spoken! Did not the Christ have to suffer these things and then enter his glory?' And beginning with Moses and all the Prophets, he explained to them what was said in all the Scriptures concerning himself. As they approached the village to which they were going, Jesus acted as if he were going farther. But they urged him strongly, 'Stay with us, for it is nearly evening; the day is almost over.' So he went in to stay with them.

When he was at the table with them, he took bread, gave thanks, broke it and began to give it to them. Then their eyes were opened and they recognized him, and he disappeared from their sight. They asked each other, 'Were not our hearts burning within us while he talked with us on the road and opened the Scriptures to us?'

They got up and returned at once to Jerusalem. There they found the Eleven and those with them, assembled together and saying, 'It is true! The Lord has risen and has appeared to Simon.' Then the two told what had happened on the way, and how Jesus was recognized by them when he broke the bread. While they were still talking about this, Jesus himself stood among them and said to them, 'Peace be with you.' They were startled and frightened, thinking they saw a ghost. He said to them, 'Why are you troubled, and why do doubts rise in your minds? Look at my hands and my feet. It is I myself! Touch me and see; a ghost does not have flesh and bones, as you see I have.' When he had said this, he showed them his hands and feet. And while they still did not believe it because of joy and amazement, he asked them, 'Do you have anything here to eat?' They gave him a piece of broiled fish, and he took it and ate it in their presence.

He said to them, 'This is what I told you while I was still with you: Everything must be fulfilled that is written about me in the Law of Moses, the Prophets and the Psalms.' Then he opened their minds so they could understand the Scriptures. He told them,

'This is what is written: The Christ will suffer and rise from the dead on the third day, and repentance and forgiveness of sins will be preached in his name to all nations, beginning at Jerusalem.'

John 20:1–29

Early on the first day of the week, while it was still dark, Mary Magdalene went to the tomb and saw that the stone had been removed from the entrance. So she came running to Simon Peter and the other disciple, the one Jesus loved, and said, 'They have taken the Lord out of the tomb, and we don't know where they have put him!' So Peter and the other disciple started for the tomb. Both were running, but the other disciple outran Peter and reached the tomb first. He bent over and looked in at the strips of linen lying there but did not go in. Then Simon Peter, who was behind him, arrived and went into the tomb. He saw the strips of linen lying there, as well as the burial cloth that had been around Jesus' head. The cloth was folded up by itself, separate from the linen. Finally the other disciple, who had reached the tomb first, also went inside. He saw and believed. (They still did not understand from Scripture that Jesus had to rise from the dead.)

Then the disciples went back to their homes, but Mary stood outside the tomb crying. As she wept, she bent over to look into the tomb and saw two angels in white, seated where Jesus' body had been, one at the head and the other at the foot. They asked her, 'Woman, why are you crying?' 'They have taken my Lord away,' she said, 'and I don't know where they have put him.' At this, she turned around and saw Jesus standing there, but she did not realize that it was Jesus. 'Woman,' he said, 'why are you crying? Who is it you are looking for?' Thinking he was the gardener, she said, 'Sir, if you have carried him away, tell me where you have put him, and I will get him.' Jesus said to her, 'Mary'. She turned toward him and cried out in Aramaic, 'Rabboni!' (which means Teacher). Jesus said, 'Do not hold on to me, for I have not yet returned to the Father. Go instead to my brothers and tell them, "I am returning to my Father and your Father, to my God and your God".' Mary Magdalene went to the disciples with the news: 'I have seen the Lord!' And she told them that he had said these things to her.

On the evening of that first day of the week, when the disciples were together, with the doors locked for fear of the Jews, Jesus came and stood among them and said, 'Peace be with you!' After he said this, he showed them his hands and side. The disciples were overjoyed when they saw the Lord. Again Jesus said, 'Peace be with you! As the Father has sent me, I am sending you.' And with that he breathed on them and said, 'Receive the Holy Spirit. If you forgive anyone his sins, they are forgiven; if you do not forgive them, they are not forgiven.'

Now Thomas (called Didymus), one of the Twelve, was not with the disciples when Jesus came. So the other disciples told him, 'We have seen the Lord!' But he said to them, 'Unless I see the nail marks in his hands and put my finger where the nails were, and put my hand into his side, I will not believe it.' A week later his disciples were in the house again, and Thomas was with them. Though the doors were locked, Jesus came and stood among them and said, 'Peace be with you!' Then he said to Thomas, 'Put your finger here; see my hands. Reach out your hand and put it into my side. Stop doubting and believe.' Thomas said to him, 'My Lord and my God!' Then Jesus told him, 'Because you have seen me, you have believed; blessed are those who have not seen and yet have believed.'

11 Caesar
His subversion of an empire

The emperor and his gospel

Some will have heard before of the child born in the Roman Empire over 2000 years ago who would change the course of history. As the child grew, his power would command the loyalty of thousands upon thousands. By the time he was in his 30s he would be seen as the fulfilment of national hopes and founder of an endless kingdom. His achievements would be considered miraculous, signs of divine authority, particularly the way he established peace in a period marked by chaos.

So significant was this man's entry into history that official proclamations, known as 'gospels', were published throughout the world in his honour. One such proclamation was inscribed on a stone tablet, and was recently uncovered in Priene on the South West coast of Turkey. It describes how the Governor of the region decreed that the year of this Saviour's birth was henceforth to be known as Year 1 of a whole new calendar system. The inscription declares:

> *God sent him as a saviour for us to make war to cease, to create peaceful order everywhere. And the birthday of this 'god' was the beginning for the world of gospels that have come to men through him. So, Paulus Fabius Maximus, the proconsul of the province of*

Asia [modern Turkey] has devised a way of honouring him, namely, that the reckoning of time for the course of human life should begin with the year of his birth.[119]

The 'saviour' I am describing is not Jesus but Gaius Octavius, otherwise known as Caesar Augustus (63 BC–14 AD), the first emperor of Rome.

If my description of Emperor Augustus sounds strangely like an account of Christ, this is not because of any spin I am giving the retelling. The language of a 'gospel' for humankind, a 'saviour' sent by God and 'peace' for the world were Roman imperial themes long before it was Christian vocabulary. And herein lies a window into a subtle but significant portrait of Jesus contained in the New Testament. The outrageous claim of the early Christians was that Jesus replaced the Roman emperor as the true Lord of the world.

The kingdom of Caesar versus the kingdom of God

The opening paragraphs of the Gospel of Luke narrate the well-known story of the birth of Christ. The text is far more than the sweet scene usually sentimentalized in Christmas cards. Throughout the text Luke borrows long established imperial terminology and, like other New Testament writers, deliberately applies it to Jesus, the Jewish Messiah descended from King David and destined to rule the world forever. The gospel of Christ is here set over and against the gospel of Caesar. Chapter 2 of Luke's Gospel begins this way:

In those days Caesar Augustus issued a decree that a census should be taken of the entire Roman world. (This was the first census that took place while Quirinius was governor of Syria.) And everyone went to his own town to register. So Joseph also went up from the town of Nazareth in Galilee to Judea, to Bethlehem the town of David, because he belonged to the house and line of David. He went there to register with Mary, who was pledged to be married to him and was expecting a child.
Luke 2:1–5

There were many censuses like this in the ancient world and, although we do not have corroboration for the one mentioned here, we do know of one conducted a decade later by the same Quirinius. The important thing to note, however, is that a census in Roman thought had nothing to do with assessing the distribution of health services or improving public transport. It was all about Roman power and wealth. It was a way for the Emperor to know how many people he ruled and how much revenue he could expect.

Against this background, the mention of the Christ-child 'belonging to the house and line of David' fires a subtle but unmistakable salvo across the bow of the imperial machinery. If this were the first time we had heard of the 'line of David', we might have glanced over the reference as trivial – a mere genealogical detail. But Luke has already told us in Chapter 1 what these references to David are all about. In the announcement to Mary about her future child we read:

> *You [Mary] will be with child and give birth to a son, and you are to give him the name Jesus. He will be great and will be called the Son of the Most High. The Lord God will give him the throne of his father David, and he will reign over the house of Jacob [i.e. Israel] forever; his kingdom will never end... So the holy one to be born will be called the Son of God.*
> ***Luke 1:31–35***

This angelic announcement to Mary recalls the fundamental Jewish hope that a descendant of King David would one day rule an eternal kingdom (discussed in Chapter 5). There can be no missing the point, then, when we arrive at Luke Chapter 2. Just as Emperor Augustus is flexing his imperial muscles around the world, Mary and Joseph are making their way to Bethlehem, the town of David, where Mary will give birth to the Messiah promised to David. The kingdom of Augustus is about to contend with the kingdom of David, the kingdom of God.

What is especially striking in terms of the clash between messianic and imperial claims is that this descendant of David, according to Luke 1:35 (above), is to be hailed 'Son of God'.

Many readers will be used to associating that title with Jesus alone. But the people of the Roman Empire – Luke's first readers – knew full well that the current bearer of that title was none other than the emperor.

As the adopted son of the deified Julius Caesar, emperor Augustus assumed the public title 'son of the god Julius'. The title then passed on to his heirs. Augustus' (adopted) son, Tiberius, was emperor from AD 14–37, for the entire period of Jesus' adulthood. He informed everyone in the empire – all 50 million of them – that he was 'son of god' by inscribing it on the most used coin of the empire. Every denarius (the labourer's daily wage) minted during his 23-year reign bore the inscription: TI(BERIVS) CAESAR DIVI AVG(VSTI) F(ILIVS): 'Tiberius Caesar, son of the god Augustus'.

For ancient readers, then, Luke's presentation of Jesus as the Son of God entitled to an eternal throne sets up an immediate and subversive contrast between the Roman emperor, with his pretensions to divine sonship, and the Davidic Messiah, God's true Son.

The emperor, the manger and the cross

Lest we get carried away with this and think the Messiah has come to do battle with Rome, the circumstances of the birth of this Son of God make clear that his will be a very different kind of kingdom. Luke's Gospel continues the Christmas narrative in these words:

> *While they were there, the time came for the baby to be born, and she gave birth to her firstborn, a son. She wrapped him in cloths and placed him in a manger, because there was no room for them in the inn.*
> ***Luke 2:6–7***

Augustus was born into privilege. Jesus was born to peasants and was laid in a 'manger', an animal feeding area. Clearly, God destined his Messiah for a very different kind of rule. This is the theme Luke wishes to strike here. The manger is a potent sign of the kind of kingship Jesus would embody in his adulthood: he would achieve his glory not through power and coercion but in humility.

Indeed, what is implied by the manger will be explicit at his cross: this emperor wins allegiance through humble sacrifice. In this context, it is worth reflecting on another passage, from the end of Jesus' life, which challenges Roman pretensions about the emperor. In the crucifixion narrative of Mark's Gospel we read:

> *With a loud cry, Jesus breathed his last. The curtain of the temple was torn in two from top to bottom. And when the centurion, who stood there in front of Jesus, heard his cry and saw how he died, he said, 'Surely this man was the Son of God!'*
> ***Mark 15:37–39***

How beautifully ironic – Mark intends us to observe – that at the moment of Jesus' death on a Roman cross, a commander in the imperial army declares the Jewish Messiah to be the 'Son of God'. What Luke hints at in the beginning of his Gospel, Mark makes plain in the climax of his Gospel: from the manger to the cross, the true emperor rules in humility and sacrifice. The values of Rome are being deliberately turned upside down. To quote Paul Barnett, an Australian New Testament historian (and former bishop):

> *That a Roman, for whom crucifixion was an unmentionable obscenity, declares a crucified Jew to be the Son of God is astonishing. Romans only applied that title to the Roman emperor, who was associated with power and triumph. But this soldier applies the title to Jesus – a poor, humiliated, crucified man. This represents an inconceivable reversal in values.*[120]

The gospel of emperor Christ

The clash between the kingdom of Christ and the empire of Rome continues through Luke's Christmas narrative, as he describes the first announcement, or 'gospel', concerning the birth of Jesus. I said earlier that sending out heralds to proclaim gospels concerning the emperor's achievements was common practice at the time of Jesus' birth. I have already quoted the Priene inscription:

> *God sent him [Augustus] as a saviour for us to make war to cease, to create peaceful order everywhere. And the birthday of this 'god' was the beginning for the world of gospels ['good news'] that have come to men through him.*

Luke 2 describes a new 'gospel' about a true 'Saviour' who brings lasting 'peace'. The heavenly herald declares to the shepherds:

> *'Do not be afraid. I bring you good news [literally: gospel] of great joy that will be for all the people. Today in the town of David a Saviour has been born to you; he is Christ the Lord.'... Suddenly a great company of the heavenly host appeared with the angel, praising God and saying, 'Glory to God in the highest, and on earth peace to men on whom his favour rests.'*
> ***Luke 2:10–14***

The point of all this is to say that the first Christians, and Luke among them, believed they were in possession of a new gospel about the true emperor of the world. His kingdom, they declared, would bring peace, not by smothering force, but by his death and resurrection, through which he would restore us to God and bind us to one another.

At times this gospel sounded like a direct challenge to Caesar, and in a sense it was. When the apostle Paul was in Thessalonica (Northern Greece) in AD 49 his message about Jesus' kingdom caused a riot. Paul's accusers in the city declared:

> *'These men who have caused trouble all over the world have now come here... They are all defying Caesar's decrees, saying that there is another king, one called Jesus.' When they [the Roman officials] heard this, the crowd and the city officials were thrown into turmoil.*
> ***Acts 17:6–8***

The Christian gospel was (and is) subversive – not in a military sense but certainly in a social, intellectual and moral sense. The gospel never said that someone else should be sitting on the throne in Rome but it did insist that someone else held the throne of the human heart and mind. Caesar was due my taxes and civil respect, said the early Christians, but he was not entitled to my love and worship, and he had no claim over my ethics. Those privileges, declared this gospel, belong to Jesus alone, the true Son of the true God.[121]

Of course, once this message was detected on the imperial radar, Rome responded by trying to eradicate the followers of Jesus, crucifying them, burning them alive and using them for sport in the Colosseum. And, yet, the movement grew. In less than three centuries, and in a way that no one can really explain, Christianity captured the heart of Rome. By AD 320 the name Caesar Augustus was a fading memory and the name *Iesous Christos*, Jesus Christ, enjoyed the allegiance of as many as half the 60 million residents of the empire, including that of the Emperor himself.[122] Imagine the feeling among believers at that time when Rome stopped producing coins inscribed 'Caesar, son of God' and started minting coins marked C-R (chi-rho), the first two letters of the word CRISTOS (Christ). Jesus was being praised in a manner once reserved for emperors. The outrageous idea put forward in the Gospels had become a reality: the kingdom, inaugurated with a manger and a cross, had conquered the empire carved out with a sword.

Reflections

The New Testament portrait of Jesus as true emperor obviously has less sting in it for us than it would for the people of the first few centuries. But the point of the portrait remains the same. The gospel of Christ, rightly understood, is still subversive. It calls on men and women to see Christ as eternal and primary and all human cultures as provisional and temporary. Seeing Christ as emperor involves doing the hardest thing of all: refusing to be a captive to one's culture.

As much as I like to think of myself as informed and clear-visioned, I am really a product of a cultural outlook that is thoroughly Western, individualistic, materialistic, monopolistic, image-obsessed, and comfort-driven. Today, we might not have an imperial machine trying to shape our lives but we have a cultural machine that more than makes up for that. Seeing Jesus as emperor calls on people to rise above the culture of their day, to sit loosely to the claims of 'empire' and give priority to the values of Christ's kingdom.

Viewing Jesus as emperor also entails conceding that no part of life is free from the claims of Christ. Whatever the practice of modern believers, historic Christianity has always insisted that Jesus does not just rule an ethereal dimension of our existence called 'religion' – our prayers and church attendance. The imperial descriptions of Jesus remind readers that he is Lord over all things religious and secular, spiritual and physical, private and public. He has claims, so the New Testament insists, over my finances, my career, my politics, my sex life, my intellect, my leisure, my ambitions and my family. In short, confessing Christ as emperor is about giving him free reign in one's life, knowing that all empires pass into oblivion while Christ's kingdom reigns eternal.

12 God
His oneness with the Almighty

Divinity by a vote?

It has been said that the doctrine of Christ's divinity, so important to the Christian church through the ages, was really just the result of a vote, and a relatively close vote at that.

As relations between Christians and pagans became increasingly tense, the fourth-century Emperor Constantine needed a political masterstroke that would bind the empire together. He found it in a theological proposal designed to blend Christian devotion to the man Jesus with the pagan worship of divinities. The emperor proposed, so the story goes, that Jesus should be regarded as divine, a god in his own right.

The plan was brilliant. Not only would it blend Christian and pagan beliefs, it would also provide Constantine with a powerful new political tool – a divine figure whose authority could not be challenged by the masses.

A great council of Roman Catholic bishops was convened in AD 325 in the city of Nicaea. The emperor put forward his idea, applied the appropriate political pressure and, with the smallest of margins, won the vote. From now on, declared the Council of Nicaea, Jesus was to be worshipped as 'true God of true God, begotten, not made, of one being with the Father', as the church's Nicene Creed (still said today) declares. The Vatican was complicit in this new vision of Jesus because it gave them more power. Now they could claim to be the custodians not only of a great moral teacher, but of an all-powerful deity.

All that was left to complete Constantine's plan was a small rewriting of the history books. With the help of the Vatican again, the emperor banned and burned the original Gospels about Jesus – those which spoke of him as merely human – and commissioned four newly edited Gospels, ones that were more supportive of the idea that Jesus was divine.

I should stop this version of the Jesus-becomes-God story before fellow believers report me to church officials and the historically informed advise my academic superiors. Almost nothing in the chapter so far could be described as factual. Indeed, readers may have recognized this account of Jesus' rise to divinity as that offered by the fictional academics, Leigh Teabing and Robert Langdon, in Dan Brown's novel *The Da Vinci Code*.

When I finally joined the 20 million others who have read this page-turner, I fully expected to find half-truth mixed with historical detail in a cleverly constructed, if somewhat controversial, account of Christian origins. Truth be told: I was secretly hoping for some cannon fodder for a series of public talks. But, as I explained to a friend who suggested I write a rebuttal of *The Da Vinci Code*, I found almost nothing recognizably historical in the book with which to even begin an historical argument.

I cannot comment on the book's treatment of sixteenth-century art, though I understand art critics are as amused by the novel as historians. However, I can say that virtually everything said in the book about the first few centuries of Christianity is fictional. At one level, I should not have expected anything different. It is a novel, after all. And yet the opening page of the book sends a rather mixed message: 'All descriptions of artwork, architecture, documents and secret rituals in this novel are accurate.' I can only imagine this statement was intended by the author as a literary device, a way of drawing readers in to Brown's world of intrigue. For, frankly, in the case of the book's account of how Jesus came to be regarded as divine, I found only one detail that could be described as accurate – and that was simply a date. The Council of Nicaea did in fact meet in the year AD 325.

Council of Nicaea (AD 325)

Beyond providing the correct date, everything Brown's characters say about this ancient council and the New Testament is either baseless or the opposite of what historians generally conclude. To begin with, the Vatican had very little presence at the great Council of Nicaea. The bishop of Rome (the Pope) did not even attend – he sent two priests in his place. Of the 250 bishops participating in the discussions, only six were Catholics. The rest were Eastern Orthodox – from Egypt, Palestine, Syria, Turkey and Greece. To describe the Nicaean Council as a Vatican conspiracy to gain power is, well, novel!

Secondly, the discussion at Nicaea was not *whether* Jesus was divine but in what manner. The council gathered, in part, to assess the views of a recent theologian named Arius. Arius had proposed a way of thinking about Jesus' divinity that fitted better with the pagan belief that what is Infinite could never be contained in what is Finite. The *fullness of God* in a man was unthinkable in Greco-Roman philosophy. Arius insisted that the divinity of Jesus was *derived from* and *subordinate to* the infinite divinity of God the Father. Jesus was thought of as a bridge between the Finite and Infinite – a much more palatable idea in pagan thought. It was precisely against Arius' concession to pagan thinking that the majority of bishops at the Nicene Council re-affirmed their belief in Jesus' full divinity.[123]

Another Dan Brown *faux pas* concerns the role of the emperor in all this. Constantine convened the council and gave the opening address but he neither chaired the eight-week meeting nor determined its theological direction. All the emperor wanted was an agreement. To quote the *Oxford Dictionary of the Christian Church*, the academic authority on such matters, 'Constantine's main interest was to secure unity rather than any predetermined theological verdict'.[124]

Actually, Constantine was a theological 'flip-flop' on this issue. Although in the interests of unity he endorsed the majority view at Nicaea and even punished bishops who rejected the council's decision, there is evidence both before and after AD 325 that he inclined toward the views of the Arians. It is testimony to how little influence the emperor had over church theology that the fourth-century church leaders rejected his preference – in both the East and the West. One could say it is testimony to the strength of Constantine's commitment to unity that he publicly endorsed, and even enforced, not a private view but the majority view, whatever that happened to be.

As for the idea that Constantine commissioned the four Gospels now in the New Testament in an effort to promote a divine Jesus, it is somewhat revealing to note that Arius and his supporters were using exactly the same Gospels. In any case, we have manuscript copies of these Gospels that predate Constantine by more than a century.[125] Even the most sceptical scholars today still date the composition of the Gospels to the first century.[126]

Jesus' divinity in the sources

Far from being a pagan invention of a fourth-century emperor, belief in Jesus' full divinity – his oneness with the Father – is found everywhere in Christian literature from the first to the fourth centuries.

Even non-Christian texts attest to the early Christian belief in Jesus' divinity. In the middle of the second century the Greek intellectual Celsus pours scorn on Jesus, saying he:

> *... tried his hand at certain magical powers, and on account of those powers gave himself the title of God.*
> ***Contra Celsum 1.32–33***

More significant is a letter from the Roman administrator Pliny to Emperor Trajan. The letter can be dated to AD 110 – two centuries before Constantine. In the letter Pliny seeks advice on whether to keep executing the followers of Jesus. He tells the emperor that his interviews with Christians revealed only the following 'crime':

> *The sum total of their guilt or error was no more than the following. They had met regularly before dawn on a determined day, and sung antiphonally (i.e. alternately by two groups) a hymn to Christ as to a god.*
> **Pliny, *Letters 10.96***

This text confirms what we know from our New Testament documents. In a departure from both Jewish and pagan thinking, the early Christians worshipped the man Jesus as the embodiment of divinity.

What is doubly fascinating is that at least two 'hymns to Christ as God', as Pliny calls them, are preserved in our earliest New Testament source – the letters of Paul. Remember, Paul's letters were composed even before the Gospels so, in historical terms, they are highly significant sources for earliest Christianity. In his letter to the Christians at Colossae (south western Turkey) Paul offers a two-paragraph poem lauding Jesus in phrases such as:

> *[Christ] is the image of the invisible God...*
> *For by him all things were created...*
> *For God was pleased to have all his fullness dwell in him*
> *[the Infinite in the Finite].*
> ***Colossians 1:15–20***

There is debate about whether Paul composed this hymn himself or merely quoted what was already a well-known song of praise. For our purposes that does not matter. All I want us to notice is that in our earliest Christian writings Jesus is already worshipped as the singular embodiment of God's invisible fullness.

Another 'hymn to Christ as God' is found in the apostle Paul's letter to the church at Philippi (northern Greece). The poetry of the Greek text cannot be seen in English translation, but most modern Bibles set the passage out in hymnic stanzas (like the following):

Your attitude should be the same as that of Christ Jesus:
Who, being in very nature God,
did not consider equality with God
something to be grasped,
but made himself nothing,
taking the very nature of a servant,
being made in human likeness.
And being found in appearance as a man,
he humbled himself and became obedient to death –
even death on a cross!
Therefore God exalted him to the highest place
and gave him the name that is above every name,
that at the name of Jesus every knee should bow,
in heaven and on earth and under the earth,
and every tongue confess that Jesus Christ is Lord,
to the glory of God the Father.
Philippians 2:5–11

There is so much we could explore in these intriguing words – particularly the theme of *Christ as servant*, which we will study in the final chapter of this book. For now, I want us to notice how the hymn begins and ends: with the claim that Christ shares the nature and name of God. Prior to Christ's entry into the world he was 'in very nature God'. He enjoyed 'equality with God', though he relinquished this status in his earthly ministry and suffering narrated in the next few sentences.

After Christ's service to humanity, declares this hymn, God 'exalted him to the highest place and gave him the name that is above every name'. The 'name' referred to here is not the name 'Jesus'; it is the name of God himself. It is the title 'Lord'. The Old Testament background of the final stanza makes that clear. In the book of Isaiah God himself declares:

By myself I have sworn, [says the Lord], my mouth has uttered in all integrity a word that will not be revoked:

'Before me every knee will bow; by me every tongue will confess.'
Isaiah 45:23

The final lines of Paul's hymn take this Old Testament statement by God and apply it to the exalted Messiah:

... that at the name of Jesus every knee should bow, in heaven and on earth and under the earth, and every tongue confess that Jesus Christ is Lord.

The promise of God's universal lordship contained in the book of Isaiah is fulfilled, says this New Testament hymn, when every knee bows before and every tongue confesses Jesus as Lord. He is the one who shares the nature and name of the Almighty.

Jesus' divinity in the Gospels

What is sung in these New Testament hymns is narrated in the New Testament Gospels. At the simplest level, we could turn to statements in the Gospel of John. In one well-loved passage, Philip pleads with Jesus for a clear account of God the Father:

Philip said, 'Lord, show us the Father and that will be enough for us.' Jesus answered: 'Don't you know me, Philip, even after I have been among you such a long time? Anyone who has seen me has seen the Father.'
John 14:8–9

The claim here is similar to that contained in the first New Testament hymn quoted above: Jesus is 'the image of the invisible God'.[127]

We could also turn to the end of John's Gospel where the doubting Thomas sees the risen Jesus and makes a confession perfectly aligned with the second hymn quoted above. Titles normally reserved for the Almighty ('God' and 'Lord') are applied to Jesus:

> *Then he said to Thomas, 'Put your finger here; see my hands. Reach out your hand and put it into my side. Stop doubting and believe.' Thomas said to him, 'My Lord and my God!' Then Jesus told him, 'Because you have seen me, you have believed; blessed are those who have not seen and yet have believed.'*
> ***John 20:27–29***

There are modern-day followers of the fourth-century Arius who try to avoid the implication of a passage like this. The Jehovah's Witnesses, for example, whom many readers will have met at their front door over the years, regard Jesus merely as an angelic being. They thus interpret Thomas' words here as an exclamation in the presence of Jesus rather than one *directed* toward him – a kind of 'Oh my God.' Unfortunately, the original Greek of the relevant sentence is perfectly clear: *eipen autō* can only mean 'said to him' ('my Lord and my God').

It is because of statements like these, along with those in the New Testament hymns quoted earlier, that the Council of Nicaea rejected the more plausible pagan belief in a semi-divine Jesus, and re-affirmed the Jesus who was 'of one being with the Father'.

The New Testament statements pointing to Jesus' oneness with God number about a dozen by my count.[128] But I want to conclude the argument of this chapter by outlining a more subtle, though perhaps more foundational, basis for the early Christian belief that Jesus was 'in very nature God'. It has to do with the topic of Chapter 8 in this book, Jesus as Temple.

Without going over the details again, readers will recall that Jesus set himself *over* and *in place of* the great Jerusalem temple – the locus of God's presence and mercy. In a huge claim to authority, he cleared the temple of its priestly merchants and when asked for a sign of his authority to do such a thing he replied that he would destroy the temple and rebuild it in three days, at which point John's Gospel adds, 'the temple he had spoken of was his body'.[129] Again, in Matthew's Gospel, Christ compared his disciples to the temple priests and said of himself, 'one greater than the temple is here'.[130] Equally revealing is that Christ boldly usurped the function of the temple whenever he handed out God's forgiveness on his own authority. The religious leaders knew exactly what this implied and protested: 'Who is this fellow who speaks blasphemy? Who can forgive sins but God alone?'[131] In short, Jesus was a mobile temple, a one man locus of the divine presence and mercy.

From the historical point of view, the early worship of Jesus as the embodiment of God is probably to be traced to Jesus' own daring identification of himself with God's dwelling place, the temple. To quote N. T. Wright, a leading British historical-Jesus scholar (a *non*-fictional character):

> *My conclusion from this brief survey of the evidence is that Jesus believed himself called to act as the new Temple. When people were in his presence, it was as if they were in the Temple. But if the Temple was itself the greatest of Israel's incarnational symbols, the conclusion was inevitable (though the cryptic nature of Jesus' actions meant that people only gradually realized what he had in mind): Jesus was claiming, at least implicitly, to be the place where and the means by which Israel's God was at last personally present to and with his people. Jesus was taking the huge risk of acting as if he were the Shekinah [divine glory] in person, the presence of YHWH [God himself] tabernacling with his people.*[132]

The doctrine of Christ's full divinity was not a pagan outcome of fourth-century politics. It was implied by Jesus himself, sung about in the earliest Christian hymns, defended at the Council of Nicaea, and has been affirmed by all mainstream believers Orthodox, Roman Catholic and Protestant ever since.

Reflections

So what are the implications of the New Testament affirmation that Jesus Christ embodied the Almighty? Let me offer an analogy, based on a true story, and then bring this chapter to a close.

Some of you may have heard before about a young woman raised in a small town outside Rio de Janeiro. Christina had always longed to experience the bright lights and party atmosphere of Brazil's famous city, but her mother had often warned her off – unemployment in the city was high; strip joints and brothels were just about the only places offering jobs to young women.

Christina did not listen. One day she packed her bags and secretly took off to the city. Terrified at what might become of her daughter, Christina's mother set out to find her. She searched the vast city in vain. Fearing the worst, she visited some of Rio's sleaziest establishments. And on the walls of these places she pinned photos of herself. On the back of each photo she wrote a simple message pleading with her daughter to come home.

Christina did eventually find herself employed in a Rio brothel. She was too ashamed to go home and, even if she wanted to, she was unsure her mother would take her back. One day, Christina was stumbling down the stairwell of one of these places when she noticed on the wall a photo of her mother. She took the image and read the message. And in that moment gazing down at her mother's image her confusion evaporated. The photo said it all. She returned home at once.

The doctrine of Christ's divinity declares that God has left a photo of himself in the world. From the first to the twenty-first centuries, Christians have claimed that in the life, teaching, miracles, death and resurrection of Jesus, we see God. In the words of the New Testament hymn quoted earlier, 'He is the image of the invisible God'.[133] Christ's life, in other words, clarifies the character and intentions of the Creator.

Throughout the centuries, this idea has brought comfort for some; for others, a challenge. For those with theological dilemmas and life experiences that have distorted their picture of God, looking to Christ – the photo of God – has brought the Almighty back into focus. There, one sees the Creator in all his grace, gentleness and love. A famous sixteenth-century theological adage stated: God is as he is toward us in Christ. In other words, what you see in Jesus is what you get with God. 'Anyone who has seen me,' says Jesus in John's Gospel, 'has seen the Father.'[134] For millions of people throughout the centuries this has been an enormous comfort.

But there has also always been a challenge in this New Testament theme. Many people through the ages have preferred to 'cherry-pick' their image of God – a little bit of this, an adjustment of that, and so on. However, if, as mainstream Christianity affirms, God has revealed himself in the life of Christ, this tendency to pick and choose is relegated to the level of wishful thinking and self-flattery. The doctrine of Christ's divinity insists that men and women are not at liberty to fashion a god of their own liking, for God has made *himself* known.

13 Servant
His preference for the lowly

The Christian blasphemy

I once gave a talk at the University of Western Sydney on the theme of the last chapter – the divinity of Christ. I focused on the crucifixion narrative and underlined for the audience the uniqueness of historic Christianity's claim that the Creator of the universe would condescend to take on flesh and suffer at the hands, and for the sake, of his creatures. After the talk the chairperson opened the floor for questions. Without blinking, a man in his mid-30s stood up and proceeded to tell the audience how preposterous was the idea that the King of the universe could be subservient to the forces of his own creation. God is all-powerful and all-knowing, he declared: how could the Almighty experience frailty and suffering!

It turned out that the man was a Muslim leader at the university and an academic. His monologue was probably the longest five minutes of my speaking career. He was very civil, but was adamant that what I had said was illogical: the Creator and Sustainer of all things could not possibly be dependent on earthly sustenance. In his mind, Jesus' need for earthly food was a knockdown argument against his divinity. More seriously, he insisted that what I had said was 'blasphemy' because I had associated infinite majesty with human weakness and servitude. Only later did I realize these were traditional Islamic arguments against the Christian understanding of Jesus. They come straight out of the Qur'an itself:

> *They do blaspheme who say, 'God is Christ, the son of Mary.' If they desist not from their word of blasphemy, verily a grievous penalty will befall the blasphemers. Christ the son of Mary was no more than an apostle. His mother was a woman of truth. They both had to eat their daily food. See how God makes his signs clear to them; yet see in what ways they are deluded.*
> ***Qur'an Sura 5:75–78***

When the chairperson invited me to respond, I did my best to address his main concerns. But it soon became obvious there was not going to be a 'winner' in this debate. Our premises were miles apart. His vision of a majestic God excluded, by definition, any notion of weakness and servanthood. My vision of God's majesty consisted precisely in the Creator's willingness to serve his creation.

I ended simply by thanking my Muslim brother for drawing to the audience's attention a profound difference between Islam and Christianity. What is blasphemous to the Muslim is glorious for the Christian: God entered his creation to serve his creatures.

Divine humility

There is no better biblical statement of this theme than the ancient Christian hymn preserved by Paul in his letter to the Philippians, discussed in Chapter 12. The text warrants quoting in full again:

> *Your attitude should be the same as that of Christ Jesus:*
> *Who, being in very nature God,*
> *did not consider equality with God*
> *something to be grasped,*
> *but made himself nothing,*
> *taking the very nature of a servant,*
> *being made in human likeness.*

And being found in appearance as a man,
he humbled himself and became obedient to death –
even death on a cross!
Therefore God exalted him to the highest place
and gave him the name that is above every name,
that at the name of Jesus every knee should bow,
in heaven and on earth and under the earth,
and every tongue confess that Jesus Christ is Lord,
to the glory of God the Father.
Philippians 2:5–11

In the history of Christianity, the theme of Christ's divinity has always been viewed from two angles. On the one hand, understanding Jesus to be 'in very nature God' has inspired believers to marvel at his majesty. They confess that he is far more than a Teacher, Healer, Saviour and Friend; he is the Lord over all and the one before whom every knee will bow.

However, Christ's divinity has often been viewed from another angle. Pondering Jesus as the embodiment of God has led believers to marvel at the divine humility: in Christ, so the Christian church has affirmed, God is seen to be far more than Creator, Sustainer and Judge; he is revealed to be the Servant, willing to put humanity's good before his own glory.

This is precisely where the accent of the above passage falls. Although it begins and ends on a note of glory, the heart of the text concerns Christ's emptying of himself to serve the needs of others. Lines 1 and 5 of the hymn highlight this mystery in an obvious way:

Who, being in very nature God,
did not consider equality with God
something to be grasped,
but made himself nothing,
taking the very nature of a servant.

According to this early Christian confession, the one who is 'in *very nature* God' took on the '*very nature* of a servant'. The parallel is deliberate and striking. Actually, there are two words for 'servant' in the original Greek. One refers to a 'servant' with rights (*diakonos*); the other refers to one without rights (*doulos*). The second is usually translated 'slave'. *This* is the term used above, and the fact that Paul introduced it with the words 'made himself nothing' suggests that he wanted to give the term its full weight – God in Christ became a 'slave'.

The English Bible translators appear to have baulked at using the word 'slave' to describe the One who is 'in very nature God'. But such theological squeamishness is completely inappropriate in Christianity. Unlike the Qur'an, the New Testament has no problem envisaging the Lord of all serving his creatures.

In any case, the language of 'slavery' comes straight from Jesus' description of his ministry. It is entirely possible this hymn found in Paul's letter to the Philippians deliberately recalls the words of Christ found in the Gospel of Mark:

> *You know that those who are regarded as rulers of the Gentiles lord it over them, and their high officials exercise authority over them [in Roman occupied Palestine, this was a visible, daily reality]. Not so with you. Instead, whoever wants to become great among you must be your servant, and whoever wants to be first must be slave [doulos] of all. For even the Son of Man [Jesus himself] did not come to be served, but to serve, and to give his life as a ransom for many.*
> ***Mark 10:42–45***

It is difficult to convey just how radical this notion would have seemed to the first disciples. In a few years Christians would be singing hymns about Christ the Servant (such as Paul recounts), but before Jesus' death and resurrection the idea that greatness consists in humble service was not on the religious radar – not in the Egyptian mystery cults, nor Greco-Roman religions, nor even in Judaism.

Recently, I was involved in a research project (sponsored by Macquarie University) exploring the origins of the virtue of *humility*. While nowadays we take for granted that humility is a desirable quality, in the ancient world this was not so.

Humility before the gods and the socially powerful was valued, but *lowering yourself before an equal* (our working definition of humility) was considered undignified. After all, one of the chief goals of ancient Mediterranean life was to attain public honour for yourself and your family.

The first writings in antiquity to emphasize humility over honour were the New Testament texts. And the reason seems clear. The radical idea at the centre of these texts was that the Messiah and Lord was also the 'slave of all'. He came not to 'be served, but to serve, and to give his life as a ransom for many'. The cross, in other words, changed everything. If the highest Lord won his greatest achievement on a shameful cross, what else could it imply than that true glory consists in humble service!

The night before his death on a cross, according to the Gospel of John, Jesus foreshadowed the servant-theme in quite a shocking way. He did for his disciples what in antiquity only a household slave would do:

> *Jesus knew that the Father had put all things under his power, and that he had come from God and was returning to God; so he got up from the meal, took off his outer clothing, and wrapped a towel around his waist. After that, he poured water into a basin and began to wash his disciples' feet, drying them with the towel that was wrapped around him. He came to Simon Peter, who said to him, 'Lord, are you going to wash my feet?' Jesus replied, 'You do not realize now what I am doing, but later you will understand.' 'No,' said Peter, 'you shall never wash my feet.' Jesus answered, 'Unless I wash you, you have no part with me.' … When he had finished washing their feet, he put on his clothes and returned to his place. 'Do you understand what I have done for you?' he asked them. 'You call me "Teacher" and "Lord", and rightly so, for that is what I am. Now that I, your Lord and Teacher, have washed your feet, you also should wash one another's feet. I have set you an example that you should do as I have done for you.'*
>
> ***John 13:3–15***

I have often heard preachers challenge their audiences with lines like: imagine if God Almighty appeared before you right now in all his glory! The implication is that we would all feel humbled. True enough, I guess, but in my opinion, more humbling by far would be the experience of these first disciples. Imagine observing the one you revered as the epitome of greatness taking off his robe, tying a towel around his waist and doing for you what you had only ever seen a slave do for his master: without gimmick or guile he washes and dries your feet.

In the context of John's Gospel, Jesus washing the disciples' feet was intended, in part, as a picture of the humble service he would perform the following day, as he suffered and died for humanity's salvation. But it was not merely a picture or a theological illustration. The washing of the disciples' feet was intended as a potent example of the Christian life itself: 'I have set you an example,' Jesus' said to his stunned disciples. Or, to quote Mark's Gospel again, 'whoever wants to become great among you must be your servant'. Christian life, as well as Christian theology, is premised upon and characterized by the servanthood Jesus showed.

The hymn of Philippians quoted earlier makes exactly the same point. The apostle Paul did not include this passage just so his readers would sing about the 'Lord' who became a 'slave'; he included it because he wanted them to embody that mystery in their daily lives. The apostle introduces the hymn in the words:

> *Do nothing out of selfish ambition or vain conceit, but in humility consider others better than yourselves. Each of you should look not only to your own interests, but also to the interests of others. Your attitude should be the same as that of Christ Jesus [and so the hymn begins]:*
>
> *Who, being in very nature God,*
> *did not consider equality with God*
> *something to be grasped,*
> *but made himself nothing,*
> *taking the very nature of a servant…*

'Christology' – the study of the person of Christ – is intimately connected to Christian living. Knowing Christ will result in living Christianly: 'your attitude', says Paul, 'should be the same as that of Christ Jesus', the Servant. It is as simple and as difficult as that!

Reflections

At various points throughout this book I have mentioned the incredible expansion of Christianity in its first three centuries. What started as a small group of Palestinian Jews soon became the largest single social movement in the empire, winning people by the irresistible force of compassion and community. To recall the conclusion of Rodney Stark, Professor of Sociology and Comparative Religion at University of Washington:

> *The notion that the gods care how we treat one another would have been dismissed as patently absurd… This was the moral climate in which Christianity taught that mercy is one of the primary virtues – that a merciful God requires humans to be merciful… This was revolutionary stuff. Indeed, it was the cultural basis for the revitalization of the Roman world.*[135]

The crowning symbol of Christian expansion – of the 'revitalization of the Roman world', as Stark puts it – was the conversion of the emperor himself, Constantine the Great (AD 272–337), who applied his new found faith to matters of state bringing far reaching benefits to ordinary citizens.[136] Somehow, the empire established by brute force had been conquered by the message of the Servant Lord.

Sadly there is another story that could be told about the Christendom that emerged in the fourth century and beyond. The faith that had won the world through service and suffering was now, after Constantine, the beneficiary of power and privilege. With the Christianization of the emperors, Christian morality began to be written into law and so was thrust upon unbelievers. Bishops began to be elevated to the status of princes and, for a time, they even became civic judges. Church and state were entwined.

By the fourth and fifth centuries, churches had acquired land and wealth way beyond their needs, and those who opposed Christ's cause found themselves excluded, silenced and worse. Now the church grew, not through the inexplicable power of words and deeds, but by the all-too-familiar means of warfare and treaty. Imperialism became the handmaiden of Christian mission, as an earthly 'Christendom' became synonymous with God's kingdom. In the twinkling of an eye, it seems, the people of the Servant King had assumed a throne of their own.

It was by no means *all* bad – and Christians can find consolation in the fact that for the first couple of centuries it was mostly very good! But, for me, the church of the fourth century and beyond provides ample proof that when Christians wield secular power for the cause of Christ they frequently cease to be recognizably Christian. For the only 'power' the historical Jesus ever granted his followers was the power to *persuade* – and this through word and service.

Epilogue
Portrait of a follower of Jesus

Belonging to the movement inspired by the man from Nazareth begins with careful reflection on the many and varied portraits of him found in the earliest sources, the texts of the New Testament. More than that, it involves allowing these images to have their intended effect. Following Jesus, then, means learning and applying the wisdom of the *Teacher*, alleviating suffering in the name of the *Healer* and trying to live out one's imperfect life within the larger, perfect life of the true *Israel*.

To be a Christian is also to bear the name (and shame) of the Christ and to fear him as the *Judge* of all injustice, including that which lies in me. At the same time, it is to adore him as the *Friend* of sinners, a *Temple* of divine presence and the *Saviour* who died for us all. As long as these portraits are held in careful balance, true believers can never be smug in their righteousness or burdened by their unworthiness.

As the risen one, Jesus is *Adam*, the progenitor of a new humanity and the guarantor of my own resurrection. With this hope, I can sit loosely to the claims of my culture knowing that all earthly empires pass into oblivion while the kingdom of the true *Caesar* reigns eternal.

Knowing Jesus, finally, involves embracing a scandalous paradox: the one in whose face we see *God* declared himself at the same time to be the *Servant* of all. No belief is more counter-intuitive or revolutionary, for, if it is true, it means that at the heart of the universe is one who values humility above status, service above power, and generosity above privilege. And if I truly believe this, nothing will ever be the same.

Notes

Notes

1 Experts have pointed out, however, that the Latin spoken in the film was tenth-century ecclesiastical Latin and the Aramaic sounded more like modern Syrian. Nevertheless, the effect was brilliant.

2 In *The Christ Files: how historians know what they know about Jesus* (Blue Bottle Books, 2006) I explore the sources and methods used by mainstream scholars to gain a plausible picture of the historical Jesus.

3 Brisbane's *Courier Mail*, 29/05/2003.

4 For some details about this scholarly game see Chapter 1 of *The Christ Files* referred to above.

5 *Apologia* is Greek for 'answer' or 'defend'.

6 Peer review, by the way, is a quality control mechanism used in most academic fields. It basically means that to get one's research published in a reputable journal it must first be read and approved by at least two international scholars (not connected to the author). Once an article is deemed worthy of publication, it will appear in the relevant journal and form part of the ongoing scholarly conversation. It will then be cited and critiqued or endorsed in any future article or monograph (scholarly book) on the topic.

7 Representative of this mainstream historical assessment of Jesus' healings is the 500-page discussion by prolific US scholar, John P. Meier (*A Marginal Jew*, vol. 2. Doubleday, 1994, pages 507–1038).

8 The United Nations World Population Profile gives the number of Christians in the world as 2,069,883,000, almost double the figure for the next largest religion, Islam (*Britannica Book of the Year, 2004*. Encyclopedia Britannica Corporation, page 280).

9 This chapter is a brief summary of my book *The Christ Files: how historians know what they know about Jesus* (Blue Bottle Books, 2006). All the references and publishing information for these sources later mentioned can be found there.

10 Mark 6:3; Acts 12:17, 15:13; Galatians 1:19; James 1:1; Jude 1.

11 If readers are in any doubt about this, they should open up any major book on the historical Jesus and they will discover that,

whereas the Greco-Roman and Jewish sources just mentioned are treated in a matter of 10–20 pages (often less), the New Testament texts provide the principal data for the remaining several hundred pages.

12 As the literature of the Christians grew, churches all around the Mediterranean decided to meet to discuss which texts were universally regarded as sacred and authoritative. A series of councils was called, climaxing in the councils of Rome (AD 382) and Carthage, North Africa (AD 397). The policy of these councils was highly conservative. Basically, they decided to embrace as Scripture only those documents that had long been recognized throughout the churches as penned by the *first generation* of Christian leaders, that is, by those whom Jesus appointed (Peter, Paul, James, etc), or by their immediate colleagues (Mark, Luke, etc.). Thus, these councils culled rather than included, leaving us with just 27 books of the New Testament (the Gospels and the letters). The other writings (e.g. Didache, Epistle of Barnabas and others) were published in separate collections and are all readily available in English translations today. One of the most authoritative books on the question of how the New Testament documents came together was written by Bruce M. Metzger of Princeton University in the US, *The Canon of the New Testament: its origin, development and significance* (Oxford University Press, 1997).

13 An explanation of these sources, complete with their dates and particular characteristics, can be found in my previously mentioned *The Christ Files* (Blue Bottle Books, 2006).

14 Tanakh is an acronym for Torah (Law), Nevi'im (Prophets) and Ketuvim (Writings) and is the typical Jewish way of referring to their sacred Scriptures.

15 Luke 6:27–28.

16 Dan Brown, *The Da Vinci Code* (Bantam Press, 2003, pages 231–34)

17 The only notable scholar to make serious use of the Gospel of Thomas and the Gospel of Peter in his study of Jesus is John Dominic Crossan (*The Historical Jesus*, Harper San Francisco, 1991). While his work is highly regarded for other reasons (his use of modern sociology, for instance, is impressive), most scholars remain dubious about his work on this point. Historian Mark Allan Powell describes well the scholarly response to Crossan: 'His whole method of operation is criticized as idiosyncratic, tendentious, and

circular. Very few, if any, scholars would accept his scheme for dating and classifying materials.' (*Jesus as a Figure of History: how modern historians view the man from Galilee*, Westminster John Knox Press, 1998, page 95).

18 Edwin A. Judge, Emeritus Professor of Ancient History and founder of the Ancient History Documentary Research Centre, Macquarie University, made this statement in his foreword to Paul Barnett's *The Truth About Jesus* (Aquila Press, 1994).

19 Syriac Manuscript Additional 14,658.

20 Talmud *baraitha Sanhedrin* 43a–b.

21 For example, James 3:1; Ephesians 4:11.

22 James Dunn, *Jesus Remembered* (Eerdmans, 2003, pages 176–77).

23 Mishnah *Yadayim* 2:3.

24 The great Scottish philosopher, David Hume (1711–1776), argued that no evidence should ever be considered strong enough to imply the occurrence of a miraculous event. Natural explanations, no matter how convoluted, must always be preferred. Hume's argument has been proclaimed loudly and repeatedly over the years but proponents of the view are yet to explain why such blanket scepticism should apply in all cases. The reason, of course, is the assumption of atheism. If there are no powers other than the known laws of physics, by definition, there can be no supernatural events. Like most assumptions, those who deny the possibility of miracles rarely admit (or even recognize) this. Theists, on the other hand, freely admit their assumption and make it the ground of their openness to the miraculous. The plausibility of the existence of god(s), they say, makes reasonable one's belief in the possibility of occurrences unrestricted by the laws of nature. It is not my intention here to demonstrate the plausibility of the existence of god(s). I am simply pointing out that how one interprets any alleged evidence for miracles is usually determined not by evidence itself but by one's prior assumptions.

25 If readers are interested in exploring the issue of Jesus' miracles in their first-century setting, let me direct you to the two most comprehensive studies of the subject in recent years: John P. Meier's *A Marginal Jew: rethinking the historical Jesus* (vol. 2), *Mentor, Message, and Miracles* (Doubleday, 1994, pages 507–1038) and Graham H. Twelftree's *Jesus, the Miracle Worker: a historical and theological study* (IVP, 1999).

26 Josephus, *Jewish Antiquities* 14.22–24; Mishnah *Taanit* 3.8.

27 Talmud *Berakot* 34b.

28 For the details of these Christian sources see *The Christ Files: how historians know what they know about Jesus* (Blue Bottle Books, 2006).

29 *Jewish Antiquities* 18.63.

30 Talmud *baraitha Sanhedrin* 43a–b.

31 John P. Meier, *A Marginal Jew: rethinking the historical Jesus*, vol. 2 (Doubleday, 1994, pages 630–31).

32 Talmud *baraitha Sanhedrin* 43a–b. See page 39.

33 Ezekiel 16 describes God as a husband whose wife, Israel, turns her back on his love and becomes a harlot.

34 *Isra-el* comes from the Hebrew words 'strive' and 'God'. The implication may be that God *strives* on behalf of his chosen people.

35 Exodus 32:1–6.

36 Numbers 14:26–35.

37 Numbers 25:1–3.

38 The period from the entry to the Promised Land to the rise of a powerful monarchic state is recounted in the Old Testament books of Joshua, Judges, Ruth, and 1 and 2 Samuel.

39 The tragic events of Israel's fall from divine favour are narrated in the Old Testament books of 1 and 2 Kings and 1 and 2 Chronicles.

40 The pleas and promises of Israel's prophets are contained in the Old Testament books of Isaiah, Jeremiah, Ezekiel, Hosea, Zechariah and others.

41 John the Baptist, an immediate forerunner of Jesus, is known to have lived as an ascetic in the wilderness region of Judea. The Essene community, responsible for the famous Dead Sea Scrolls, likewise shared a strict monastic existence in the desert wilderness.

42 Exodus 32:1–6; Numbers 25:1–3.

43 For example, Matthew 4:18–22: 'As Jesus was walking beside the Sea of Galilee, he saw two brothers, Simon called Peter and his brother Andrew. They were casting a net into the lake, for they were fishermen. "Come, follow me," Jesus said, "and I will make you fishers of men." At once they left their nets and followed him.

'Going on from there, he saw two other brothers, James son of Zebedee and his brother John. They were in a boat with their father Zebedee, preparing their nets. Jesus called them, and immediately they left the boat and their father and followed him.'

44 The importance of 'twelve' is underlined several times throughout the Old Testament. See, for example, Genesis 17:20; Exodus 28:21; Numbers 17:1–3; Joshua 4:1–7, among many others.

45 Graham Stanton, *The Gospels and Jesus* (Oxford University Press, 2003, page 201).

46 Any Protestants who think I am being unfair at this point should take the time to read the reformer Martin Luther's 1543 publication *The Jews and Their Lies* available today in *Luther's Works*, vol. 38 (Fortress Press, 1971, pages 268–93). How Luther ever wrote this document when he had New Testament passages like Romans 9:1–5 and 11:1–32 in front of him (and Romans was his favourite biblical book!) is a mystery.

47 Many readers will wonder why this point is worth making. The reason is simple. It was once argued by scholars that Jesus' Messiah-status was only proposed in the decades *after* his death – it was not the view of his first followers and certainly not the view of Jesus himself. The Gospel writers, these critics said, wrote a Messiah-story back into their presentation of Jesus. Without Paul's letters this argument might just have worked (though many pointed out its weaknesses even on the evidence of the Gospels). However, the fact that the title Christ had already begun to morph into a kind of surname just 20 years after Jesus' death suggests that the practice of calling Jesus *the Messiah* must have begun much, much earlier, with his immediate circle of followers. N. T. Wright, British New Testament scholar, recently reiterated this point in his monumental book *The Resurrection of the Son of God* (SPCK, 2004, pages 553–63).

48 Suetonius, *Life of Claudius* 25.4; Tacitus, *Annals* 15.44. For a discussion of these passages see chapter 2 of *The Christ Files: how historians know what they know about Jesus* (Blue Bottle Books, 2006).

49 Josephus, *Jewish Antiquities* 20.200. For a discussion of both of these Josephan passages see Chapter 3 of *The Christ Files: how historians know what they know about Jesus* (Blue Bottle Books, 2006).

50 There were probably between five and eight million Jews in the first century, most of whom lived outside the Holy Land.

51 The United Nations World Population Profile gives the number of Christians in the world as 2,069,883,000 spread across all 238 listed countries (*Britannica Book of the Year, 2004*. Encyclopedia Britannica Corporation, page 280).

52 Unhappy with Roman rule of the Holy Land, many Jewish freedom fighters resorted to sporadic guerrilla warfare in an attempt to oust the wicked pagans. Several of these movements had messianic hopes, believing they were destined to establish God's kingdom over the world. Key references to Jewish resistance fighters can be found in Josephus' writings including *Jewish Antiquities* 18.3–10; 18.23–24; 20.5; *Jewish War* 2.117–18; 2.160–65.

53 Mark 1:43–44; Mark 8:29–30.

54 Acts 7:54–60.

55 Acts 12:1–2.

56 Josephus, *Jewish Antiquities* 20.200.

57 1 Clement 5:1–7; Eusebius 2.25.5–6.

58 Mark 8:36.

59 Similar statements from Israel's prophets can be found in Isaiah 10:1–3, Jeremiah 2:31–37, Amos 5:1–27, Zechariah 7:8–14. The other great sin that brought divine judgment down upon Israel was the worship of false gods. Both themes – Israel's idolatry and oppression of the needy – are frequently found together in the same prophetic denunciation (e.g. Jeremiah 2:26–37).

60 To provide just a few examples for curious readers: Matthew 7:21–23; Matthew 13:36–43; Luke 13:22–30; John 5:25–30.

61 Luke 10:13–15.

62 In a climactic scene of Luke's Gospel Jesus does in fact weep over a city (Jerusalem) which rejected him: Luke 19:41–44.

63 Some Christian commentators have interpreted the mention of 'brothers' in this passage 'whatever you did for one of the least of these brothers', to mean that the followers of Christ are to assist *only* fellow believers. To my mind, that interpretation sails dangerously close to the kind of parochialism Jesus condemned in his famous Parable of the Good Samaritan (Luke 10:25–37) where he insisted that compassion is to be shown across the religious and racial divide.

64 Among others see Luke 15:1–32; Luke 18:9–14.

65 Luke 6:36.

66 One Old Testament passage sets the sin of neglecting the Creator right alongside the sin of mistreating the oppressed (Jeremiah 2:26–37). In the New Testament, Romans 1:18–20 also underlines the point that refusing to honour the Creator merits divine judgment.

67 Jesus' words on this theme are worth quoting: 'Hearing that Jesus had silenced the Sadducees, the Pharisees got together. One of them, an expert in the law, tested him with this question: "Teacher, which is the greatest commandment in the Law?" Jesus replied: "Love the Lord your God with all your heart and with all your soul and with all your mind. This is the first and greatest commandment. And the second is like it: Love your neighbour as yourself. All the Law and the Prophets hang on these two commandments"' (Matthew 22:34–40).

68 It is worth observing that in the famous Parable of the Prodigal Son (Luke 15:11–32) Jesus describes the sinner as a son living at a distance from and in defiance of his father (i.e. God).

69 Acts 6:1–7.

70 Romans 15:24–27; 1 Corinthians 16:1–4; 2 Corinthians 8–9.

71 Eusebius, *Ecclesiastical History* 6.43.11.

72 Emperor Julian, Letter 22, *To Arcacius, High priest of Galatia* (*The Works of the Emperor Julian* vol. 2. Loeb Classical Library 157, pages 67–73). Another letter on the same theme is *Fragment of a Letter to a Priest* (*The Works of the Emperor Julian*, vol. 2. Loeb Classical Library 29, pages 337–38).

73 Households in the upper 20 per cent income range – households earning $100,000 or more before tax – spend on average $344 a year on charitable giving. That works out to just one-third of a per cent of earnings (0.33 per cent), or 33c per $100.

74 'Message and Miracles' in *The Cambridge Companion to Jesus*, Cambridge University Press, 2001, p. 69.

75 *The Rise of Christianity*, Harper Collins, 1997, pp. 209–215).

76 The incident appears also in Luke 19:28–40 and Mark 11:1–10.

77 The annual temple tax was one half-shekel, or the equivalent of a denarius – about $50–100 in modern Australian terms (US$43–86). The silver content of shekels produced in Tyre and Jerusalem was generally higher than that of Roman denarii (90 per cent and 80 per cent respectively), so the temple officials ruled that only Tyrian silver was acceptable for the annual tax.

78 The Old Testament text of Leviticus 5:7 stipulates: 'If he cannot afford a lamb, he is to bring two doves.'

79 Isaiah 11:4.

80 The accusation reappears in Matthew 27:39–40 in the crowds' mockery of Jesus on the cross: Those who passed by hurled insults at him, shaking their heads and saying, 'You who are going to destroy the temple and build it in three days, save yourself! Come down from the cross, if you are the Son of God!'

81 N. T. Wright, *The Challenge of Jesus* (IVP, 1999, pages 113–14).

82 The above true story was pieced together after the author's own research at the NSW State Archives (2 Globe Street, the Rocks, Sydney).

83 Tench's diary was recently reprinted as *Watkin Tench 1788: edited and introduced by Tim Flannery* (The Text Publishing Company, 1996). Peyton's letter is quoted on pages 68–69.

84 The saviour theme emerges strongly in L, the letters of Paul and the Gospel of Mark. Matthew and Luke (who used Mark's Gospel as a source) both endorse and expand the saviour theme found in Mark. Matthew's and Luke's shared source, Q, does not emphasize Jesus' role as saviour. This is probably partly explained by the fact that Q was not a narrative portrait of Jesus but a collection of his sayings.

85 A very early credal statement about Jesus as saviour from judgment appears in one of Paul's first extant letters: '...you turned to God from idols to serve the living and true God, and to wait for his Son from heaven, whom he raised from the dead – Jesus, who rescues us from the coming wrath' (1 Thessalonians 1:9–10).

86 Matthew 25:31–46; Luke 16:19–31.

87 This point is made clear in the famous Parable of the Prodigal Son (Luke 15:11–32). There, in a metaphor about the sinner, Jesus tells how a young son (the sinner) offended his father (God) by demanding the family inheritance and then leaving home to spend his father's goods on himself. The son wanted everything the father had to offer; he just did not want the father himself. That is what a sinner is, according to Jesus.

88 Luke 7:50.

89 The Old Testament narrative can be read in Exodus 12.

90 1 Corinthians 1:18.

91 Tacitus, *Annals* 44.2–5

92 Talmud *baraitha Sanhedrin* 43a–b.

93 Lucian, *Peregrinus* 11–13.

94 Cicero, *In Verrem* 2.5.168.

95 The definitive book on ancient crucifixion and its relevance to Christianity was written almost 30 years ago by University of Tübingen Professor Martin Hengel, *Crucifixion* (SCM, 1977).

96 Pinchas Lapide, *The Resurrection of Jesus: a Jewish perspective* (Wipf and Stock, 1982, pages 125–26).

97 In 1998, Oxford University Press published the papers of an international scholarly symposium on the topic of Christ's resurrection (*The Resurrection: an interdisciplinary symposium on the resurrection of Jesus*, Oxford University Press, 1998). Summaries of the papers are available online at www.oxfordscholarship.com. Scholars of all persuasions would agree that the most important book written on the topic of Christ's resurrection is the massive recent volume by British New Testament historian N. T. Wright (*The Resurrection of the Son of God*, SPCK, 2003).

98 One famous dying-and-rising god is the Egyptian deity Osiris who is revived by his wife (who is also his sister) Isis. The two then make love and give birth to other divinities. At no point in these myths were ancient pagans implying that such a thing happens within time and space. This was a reality of the divine world whose earthly reflection is not bodily resurrection but the renewal of agricultural harvest and human fertility.

99 In Greco-Roman thought the afterlife is always non-physical – the soul remains, the body decays. This is fundamental to the pagan outlook. Physical existence is weak, corruptible and only a poor reflection of the ultimate, non-bodily Reality.

100 To this day the future resurrection of the dead is a part of the official daily prayers of Orthodox Jews: see the famous *Shemoneh Esrei 2* in the Siddur (Jewish Prayer Book).

101 The New Testament describes the death of John the Baptist in just this way. As one killed by Rome's puppet king, Herod Agrippa, John is lauded as a pious Jewish martyr. See, for example, Mark 6:17–29.

102 James Dunn, Emeritus Professor of New Testament at the University of Durham, has recently emphasized this point in *Jesus Remembered*, (Eerdmans, 2003, pages 836–38).

103 Surprisingly, Matthew's Gospel provides the first reference to the Jewish leadership's counter-claim that the disciples stole the body (Matthew 28:12–15). This is the best kind of evidence since it is unthinkable that a Gospel writer would invent a counter-claim and put it into his work, sowing seeds of doubt among his readers. Matthew mentions the point because he wants to refute a widely circulating slander against the Christians.

104 I describe this as a popular explanation because no mainstream academic that I know of considers this even remotely plausible. Only a (very) few sensationalist scholars have attempted to recycle this argument (e.g. Barbara Thiering, *Jesus the Man*, Double Day, 1992, pages 116–20).

105 AD 33/34 is the date of Paul's first visit to Jerusalem after his conversion (Acts 9:26–31) in AD 31/32 (Jesus' death being dated in April AD 30). According to Galatians 1:18–19 Paul stayed with the apostle Peter during this 15-day visit and also met with James the brother of Jesus. Paul must have received much first-hand information about Jesus during this time (filling out what he claimed had been revealed to him personally by the risen Jesus: Gal 1:16). The creed Paul says he 'received' (1 Corinthians 15:3) is most likely to have been passed on to him during this visit. For those interested in such chronological questions, the scholarly benchmark is the book by Rainer Riesner, Professor of New Testament at Tübingen University (Germany): *Paul's Early Period: chronology, mission strategy, theology* (Eerdmans, 1998).

106 James Dunn, *Jesus Remembered* (Eerdmans, 2003, page 826).

107 Matthew 28:1–10; Mark 16:1–8; Luke 24:10–11; John 20:14–18.

108 Josephus, *Jewish Antiquities* 4.219. A similar point of view is reflected in Mishnah *Shabuot* 4.1.

109 James Dunn, *Jesus Remembered* (Eerdmans, 2003, page 833).

110 Another example is worth mentioning. It used to be argued that the Gospels' empty tomb stories were devised to stress the *bodily* nature of Christ's resurrection against an emerging Gnostic heresy that denied the physicality of Jesus. The argument always suffered from lack of evidence for Gnosticism in the first century

– it was a second-century heresy. But more tellingly, if this account of things were correct, the Gospels have done a dreadful job of underlining the physical dimension of Jesus post-resurrection. As anyone who knows the Gospels will tell you, one of the strange features of the empty tomb/resurrection accounts is the way Jesus is unrecognizable one minute then recognizable the next, the way he disappears from one group of disciples only to reappear in another (e.g. Luke 24:15–31, 36–43). The Gospels do mention that Jesus ate with his followers after the resurrection (which presumably implies a bodily reality) but they make no attempt to expunge the more super-bodily aspects of Jesus' resurrection life.

111 We should probably add to this a third conclusion (also accepted by mainstream scholars). Several of the key witnesses endured ill treatment and martyrdom rather than give up their claims about Jesus. The deaths of the apostles James, Peter and Paul and that of James the brother of Jesus were discussed in Chapter 5. The historical sources for these martyrdoms are Acts 12:1–2; Josephus, *Jewish Antiquities* 20.200; 1 Clement 5:1–7; Eusebius, *Ecclesiastical History* 2.25.5–6. It is true that fanatics regularly give their lives for a cause they believe in. The difference with the first disciples, of course, is that they were in a position to know whether their 'cause' was in fact based on a fabrication. Reflection on this point has led even the most sceptical to concede that the apostles really did think they saw Jesus alive. The body-snatching theory thus has very few adherents among professional historians.

112 Many of those who deny the possibility of a resurrection surmise that the apostles experienced either religious visions or grief induced hallucinations. Both explanations have their problems – e.g. the lack of modern parallels involving multiple visionary recipients on multiple occasions – but they remain the most cogent and popular of the non-resurrection interpretations of the historical data.

113 Graham Stanton, *The Gospels and Jesus* (Oxford University Press, 2003), page 291.

114 Sometimes they said the resurrection was God's vindication of a prophet wrongly treated (Acts 3:13–15). Often, they held it up as proof that Jesus was the Son of God, the Messiah (Romans 1:2–4).

115 See, for example, Isaiah 65:17–25.

116 The story of Adam is told in Genesis 1:27–4:1.

117 Classical Hindu descriptions of the eternal, bodiless soul (*atman*) after death may be found in the *Katha Upanishad* 2.14–3.17 (*Hindu Scriptures*, University of California Press, 1996, 173–76). While Buddhism rejects the notion of an eternal *atman*, its idea of *nirvana* is fundamentally bodiless. For an excellent exposition of this theme from the Buddha's own lips see Aggi-Vacchagottasutta (*Discourse to Vacchagotta on Fire*), Majjhima-Nikaya 72, from the Sutta Pitaka (*The Collection of the Middle Length Sayings*, vol. 2. The Pali Text Society, 1989, 162–67 pages).

118 In addition to the passage from Romans quoted above, see Isaiah 65:17–25 in the Old Testament and Revelation 20:11–21:5 in the New Testament.

119 The most complete copy of the decree comes from the Priene inscription (which is referenced as OGIS 2, 458), but fragmentary copies of the documents and accompanying letter for the decree also exist. For these see Danker, FW Benefactor: *Epigraphic Study of a Graeco-Roman and New Testament Semantic Field* (Clayton Publishing House, 1982, pages 215–27).

120 Paul Barnett, *The Servant King: reading Mark today* (Aquila Press, 1991, page 298)

121 Other New Testament writers develop the theme of Christ's lordship over Roman imperial claims (e.g. Philippians 1:27–2:11, 1 Peter 3:14–22, Revelation 13–19). Entire books have been written on the topic. See, for example, Richard A. Horsley and Neil Asher Silberman, *The Message and the Kingdom: how Jesus and Paul ignited a revolution and transformed the ancient world*, (Grosset/Putnam, 1997). I do not agree with everything in this book but it helpfully underscores the increasing scholarly interest in the subversive nature of earliest Christianity. Much more accessible is the book by British scholar N.T. Wright, *What Saint Paul Really Said* (Lion, 1997). Chapters 3 and 5 contain an excellent account of the way the apostle Paul sets Jesus over and against the Roman emperor.

122 The extent and rate of Christian expansion in the first three centuries – along with the figure cited above – are outlined in Rodney Stark's *The Rise of Christianity* (Harper Collins, 1997 pages 3–27).

123 In the end, only two of the 250 bishops in attendance sided with Arius and refused to sign the agreed statement.

124 F.L. Cross and E.A. Livingstone (editors), *Oxford Dictionary of the Christian Church* (Oxford University Press, 1997, page 1144).

125 For example, Papyrus 75 is dated AD 200 and is housed in Switzerland's Bibliotheca Bodmeriana (19–21 route du Guignard, Cologny, Switzerland).

126 Martin Hengel of the University of Tübingen (Germany) has written a very important book on how, when and why the four Gospels came to be revered in all quarters of the early church: *The Four Gospels and the One Gospel of Jesus Christ* (Trinity Press, 2000).

127 Colossians 1:15.

128 Matthew 1:23, 28:18–20; John 1:1, 14; 10:32–38, 14:9, 20:27–29; Romans 8:9–11; 1 Corinthians 8:5–6; 2 Corinthians 13:14; Philippians 2:6–11; Colossians 1:15–20; Revelation 22:12–13.

129 John 2:13–22.

130 Matthew 12:5–6.

131 Luke 5:20–21.

132 N.T. Wright, *The Challenge of Jesus* (IVP, 1999, pages 113–14).

133 Colossians 1:15.

134 John 14:9.

135 Rodney Stark, *The Rise of Christianity* (Harper Collins, 1997 pages 209–215).

136 Not only did Constantine humanize the criminal law and the law of debt, he also eased the conditions of slaves and, importantly, introduced imperial financial support for children of poor families, the effect of which was to greatly reduce the common practice of abandoning unwanted babies. See F.L. Cross and E.A. Livingstone (editors), *Oxford Dictionary of the Christian Church* (Oxford University Press, 1997, pages 405–406). An authoritative and accessible account of Constantine's conversion and its implications for the church may be found in the final two chapters of Oxford historian Robin Lan Fox's *Pagans and Christians* (Knopf, 1987, pages 609–681). The book is magnificently subtitled: *Religion and the religious life from the second to the fourth century* AD *when the gods of Olympus lost their dominion and Christianity, with the conversion of Constantine, triumphed in the Mediterranean world.*